No Fences

No _ences

it started with a plastic pony

A MEMOIR

NITA HORN

WITH DONNA HOWELL & ALLIE ANDERSON

DEFENDER

CRANE, MO

No Fences:
It Started with a Plastic Pony…A Memoir

Defender
Crane, MO 65633
©2016 by Thomas and Juanita Horn
A collaborative work by Juanita Horn, Donna Howell, and Allie Anderson.
All rights reserved. Published 2016.
Printed in the United States of America.

ISBN: 978-0-9964095-3-7

A CIP catalog record of this book is available from the Library of Congress.

Cover design by Jeffrey Mardis.

To Father God, Jesus Christ, and the Holy Spirit:
My deepest gratitude toward Him who saved me.
To my husband and best friend Tom ("Joe"): Thank you for being my
greatest cheerleader, supporting all my horsie dreams,
and for recognizing they were my divine calling.

To my children—Allie, who has always been my "Howdy Neighbor"
and still is; Joe, who graciously allows me to be his drummer, and has
since he was big enough to hold a guitar; Donna, who as a toddler
once sold me out for a bowl of ice cream, but has made up for it many
times and again, including her collaborative work on this memoir:
Thank you, sweet kids, for your dedication to the adventures, for never
giving me more drama then I could handle, and for growing up to
become amazing individuals and devoted followers of Christ.

To my mother: Thank you for all your sacrifices, even to your own
hurt, and for your struggles in raising us kids in a domestically
challenged home. We have shared many of these moments together,
and you have your own memoirs to write.

To Gene and Evelyn, "Grammaw and Grandpa" Fuller, Floyd
and Joann Osban, Paul and Leona Holt, Faith and Mr. Campbell, and
all the other saints in that little modest church where God first planted
us: Though some of you have gone on, your faith and spiritual
example is still paving the way for the rest of us.

To "Stinky Tink," a frumpy little miniature horse who taught me how to really listen by watching her grow beyond her abusive past, and who has helped me do the same: Thanks for everything you are, and for everything you have been to me since the beginning.

For my wonderful grandchildren: I look forward to watching you follow God's leading in your own unique dreams. Please know God will complete the good work in you that *He* started.

In memory of my baby sister Althia, who was taken from us early on: I have deeply missed you. Keep Lightning and Rosie at the ready until we will meet again on the other side.

In memory of my dear friends and mentors, Henrietta Stewart and Merriam Holmes: You were both full of grace and godly wisdom. Though you now reside with "Father God" (as Merriam always called Him), your amazing example of unconditional love will be with me forever.

A prayer for the reader:
May you find God's calling upon your life, may you look to God to help you answer the call, and may you trust in Him to help you fulfill it. Keep this verse close to your heart always:
"For I know the plans I have for you," declares the Lord, "plans to prosper you and not to harm you, plans to give you hope and a future."
Jeremiah 29:11

Contents

Foreword ix

Introduction: So… What's Your Secret? 1

Chapter 1: Lightning, Rosie, and Flying Carpets 9

Chapter 2: Coco 29

Chapter 3: The Pink Pony 41

Chapter 4: The Muddy Steed 63

Chapter 5: Shorty and the Little One 85

Chapter 6: The Bronze Clock 103

Chapter 7: Sundance 123

Chapter 8: Five Big Horses and One Big Injury 145

Chapter 9: Whispers 171

Conclusion: So… What's Your Shape? 197

Whispering Ponies Ranch Retreat Center 211

Foreword

By Thomas R. Horn

I was glad when my wife Nita finally said "yes" to writing this memoir, though—I must admit—the final product is much deeper and more thoughtful than I had expected. I laughed out loud, shuddered, and even cried as the tragedy and triumphs of this beautiful woman's extraordinary journey unfolded.

This book follows Nita from a hardship-stricken little girl with her secondhand plastic ponies and romanticized dreams to the catastrophic death of her father and sister; to the day she held a picture of a dad she had barely known and introduced him to her baby boy; to being a pastor's wife, a state director for a women and girls ministry, a successful businesswoman, and eventually building the 150-acre Whispering Ponies Ranch (a therapy animal training center and retreat facility through which children and adults find healing). Nita's willingness to share these most sensitive recollections—to publically expose her heart with its complicated moments—was not something I saw coming. Of course, I've privately understood all too well the significance of her life, as we've loved each other and been together since we were teens growing up in the small town of El Mirage, Arizona.

I still love Nita, even though in this narrative she sometimes exposes what a self-confident, cocky little stinker (and sometimes jerk) I was as a young man. *You may not be able to get the image of me on a horse stuck chest deep in the mud out of your head!*

Moving and sentimental in its storyline, *No Fences* is unlike any memoir you'll ever read. Its sacred and treasured memories of loss, tears, laughter, personal identity, struggle, dreams, and eventual success (which have been hidden from public scrutiny for decades), are often gripping—providing a searing story of a sweet, broken, yet resilient sister, daughter, wife, and mother who took on the worst of circumstances and never lost sight of the vision God gave her as a child.

So... What's Your Secret?

*A*ll people are born into a set of circumstances that shapes who they become. The way we are raised, the adults who make unforgettable impressions on us in our youth, the support we receive, the *lack* of support we receive, the friends we surround ourselves with, the schools we attend, the churches we visit...all of these factors play a role in determining the way we react to others and the decisions we make going forward.

As we grow and continue to develop, the mold we fall into resettles over and over again, allowing change as we mature. The result of this human reality is that each of us, as we are being molded, is pressured to fit into uncomfortable new shapes—requiring of us that we either adapt or become stunted in our growth, unwilling to expand to something new.

For some, this mold is gentle: The edges are soft and inviting, and people flock to these personality types for comfort and internal rest. For others, this mold is callous: The edges are harsh and sharp, the walls are raised protectively, and others are only allowed to get so close. And still, for a number of us, this mold is quirky: The edges swirl around sporadically, and people are never sure what to expect when approaching these types.

This mold may, for some, be ideal. As the external and internal pressures of life continue to extend or shrink who we are, happiness is always found in growth. However, for many, this process of change is uncomfortable, and even when we want to show willingness to adapt, to become a better "self," the requirements of the change demand a lot out of us, and it can be both exhausting and discouraging on the journey to maturity. But what we appear to be on the outside is not an accurate depiction of who we are at the center, nor is it an indicator of all we are capable of or what truly drives us. Our dreams, aspirations, goals, wishes, passions, and desires are not silenced within, even when we conform to what we are expected to be. From every angle and aspect, an outside view of every mold only represents what each individual is allowing us to see.

I recently watched an online video that a friend had sent to me. At the start, a man with a violin stood at the front of his orchestra in an absolutely beautiful room decorated with ornate golden structures and sparkling chandeliers. This man, André Rieu, a renowned Dutch violinist and musical conductor, faced his audience to relate a most fascinating story.

He began by telling his audience that he had a surprise for them. A few months prior to this concert, a phone call had come in to his New York office, one from a man so famous and celebrated that the call had not been dismissed, like so many others. Throughout his career, Rieu explained, he had frequently been inundated with phone calls and emails from aspiring musicians who had composed orchestral pieces they hoped Rieu would consider having his orchestra perform. (To do so would be a great honor, indeed.) *This* request—from a man whose name was so well known throughout the world that Rieu admitted to almost fainting when his co-staffer had announced the call—was worth paying attention to. Rieu had agreed to take the call, and went on to explain that the person on the other end of the phone had been a very nice man who had immediately established a good rapport. The voice on the line had been one of Hollywood's all-time greatest stars, who, before becoming an actor, had composed a waltz that had never before been played, and thus, had never been heard by a single soul.

The score had remained a secret for fifty years.

Now ready to reveal his sacred score to the world through only the most trusted of conductors and performers, the actor had contacted Rieu with the proposal. Rieu, of course, had accepted this mission.

This waltz, this *secret*, would be revealed that night in Vienna.

Before beginning, Rieu announced that the original composer of this breathtaking piece had flown in from Los Angeles to be present for the experience: the moment his beautiful waltz would be heard in its completion before mankind for the first time since its mysterious composition fifty years before.

The actor's name was then announced, and he stood to greet the anticipating audience with warmth. The audience, as well as every member of the orchestra, stood to honor this amazing and talented man with applause and excitement.

It was Anthony Hopkins.

Just when it seemed that the moment of mutual appreciation would and could go on forever—both from the grateful Hopkins as well as the audience who would be blessed by his musical gift that night—Rieu announced the name of the piece: "And the Waltz Goes On."

Like many, I'm sure, I was curious to hear how the star of such movies as *Hamlet*, *The Hunchback of Notre Dame*, *The Silence of the Lambs*, *Bram Stoker's Dracula*, and *Beowulf* would fare as an artist of musical composition, since his role in the world is so directly connected to the art of acting.

With no further ado, Rieu turned to his orchestra and lifted his hand, bringing it down tenderly as the first note of the piece bled into the symphony hall.

As the camera panned the elaborate room, sweet staccato strings welcomed a haunting and warm melody in an unexpected and nontraditional chord progression that immediately crept across my consciousness like a ballerina executing a perfect pirouette for the first time. The sound, this incredible tune, inspired mental imagery of two young and innocent Victorian lovebirds exchanging glances from across a dance floor, lost in the moment, carefully and slowly advancing to grasp hands in a waltz that would whisk them away in the throes of salubrious romance. I could almost see the story unfolding in my mind as the notes kissed the air.

As the tune slowly picked up speed, the rest of the orchestra joined in the fray, bringing the full force of the song with rich, graceful, boisterous ballroom glamour, the likes of which I had never before heard. As the first of many crescendos was reached, my attention was drawn from the imaginary lovers in my mind to the most important member of the audience.

There is no describing Anthony Hopkins' expression. For fifty years, he had been an actor, known to the world by merely one dimension of his potential, and for fifty years, he had waited for the right time, the right person, the right *circumstances*, to bring his hidden talent as a masterful composer into the world…and that night was the night it would happen.

He sat and listened, watching both the orchestra and those around him as everyone swayed back and forth, surrendering to the unseen energy that compelled them not only to *hear* the music, but to *live* it. Although the song had never been heard before in its fullness even by the composer, himself, Hopkins' head lifted and lowered melodically as his eyebrows rose in anticipation of the climactic notes he had for so long heard only in his imagination.

Toward the end of the video, Hopkins' beaming smile unveiled his internal bliss. His happiness was undeniable, as if his soul were soaring right along above the heads of the audience in a dance he had danced in secret for decades. He didn't dare close his eyes. He had spent too many years waiting for this moment, and it was clear that he didn't want to miss a thing. At the final note, his chin lifted for the finale, and when the song had finally been completed, only then was he able to shift from his inner rapture and into an outward gratitude for those who had partici-pated in making his dream a reality. As the audience cheered, he stood and clapped and kissed his wife, mouthing the words "thank you" to all around him.

He was a happy man.

I can see it now: Young Anthony in his bedroom while nobody was watching, bowing to his invisible partner and swirling about his bed humming a waltz so powerfully ingrained in his core being that he couldn't help but be swept away by the fantasy that the tune inspired.

Then, off to acting school to become his *outer* self, his *outer* mold, his *outer* shape…the Anthony the world would see.

How many "selfs" are you? What mold defines you to those who observe your capabilities? How many waltzes have you danced when nobody was looking? What secret dreams do you continue to grasp onto, hoping that someday your life will have the purpose you feel it was born to have?

When I was a little girl, I dreamed of someday owning horses. To me, they were nothing less than enchanting. I role-played that I was both the horse and the rider more times than I can remember. I would wake up with horses in my thoughts and go to bed with them still there. They could do no wrong. I dreamed of them constantly, and prayed for them often throughout my childhood.

When the children in my neighborhood were available to play, I would place them in my "carriage" (a little red wagon), and with the wagon tied around my waist by a rope and hands slapping a clippity-clop rhythm against my thighs, I "galloped" about the streets, more than willing to sacrifice physical comfort in exchange for *becoming* the thing I most dreamed about. When my younger sister and I played imaginatively, a horse was always the central character. Whenever I was able to choose a toy, it was always a stuffed horse, a plastic pony, or a brush for my stuffed horse's mane—any item that could be used for further role-playing *as* a horse.

As I grew, and as my mold shifted from one form to another, I couldn't purge the inner "horsie" that drove me to believe that one day, one blessed day, I would look out my window and see these majestic creatures whipping their manes in the sunshine of my backyard. Even wild horses, themselves, could not drag these thoughts from my mind.

My waltz played on.

But as with all little girls and their dreams, growing up was inevitable. Mom and Dad were always moving from place to place, and owning an animal of that size and with that level of caretaking responsibility wasn't realistic.

But my waltz played on.

Soon, as a young wife to a dedicated preacher, I had responsibilities to my husband, my children, and our ministry, and these were far higher on my priority list than playing ponies.

But my waltz played on.

Once in a while, I would find myself too driven by my dreams to ignore it. I brought home a horse now and again, but I was never able to keep it. Our finances were always tight, the kids needed my attention, or we were moving (again)… You name it. There was always a reason that I wasn't supposed to have any prancing beauties in my backyard.

But my waltz played on…

Many times throughout the years I have faced the unrelenting truth that I simply was not meant to have horses. What a silly dream, anyway, right? Some people grow up dreaming to end world hunger, fight for what's right, take a stance, change people's lives, or invent something humanity cannot live without. *These* were the dreams that mattered. Having horsies to scratch on and ride would be, at best, a hobby…but not a real vision for life-meaning. Not something that would help *people* in the light of eternity—a main concern that I had felt for years to be at the very forefront of my mind.

How could I have *ever* known, that with God's correct timing, and only under circumstances that He foresaw—after the reshaping of my mold—I would not only *have* horses, but I would use them for my life-long calling: reaching the lost and struggling people who could only be reached by unorthodox means.

The following is not only the story of the horses in my life and the lessons learned by knowing them, but the story of how God used a little girl playing "pony rides" with her sister and neighborhood friends to shape the crescendo of my dream: Whispering Ponies Ranch.

And the waltz goes on.

1

Lightning, Rosie, and Flying Carpets

*W*hat's the story?" six-year-old Althia asked.

"Oh I gotta really good one," eight-year-old Nita answered with a grin.

It had been weeks, and maybe months, since any of the farm animals had eaten. Hunger bit at them from the inside, delivering them into a delirious state of mind from which they feared they would never return. Survival looked bleak. They were starving, freezing, filthy, and beyond hope. Despite the mooing, neighing, bleating, clucking, and oinking that had poured out of the cave entrance for days in a sad and feeble cry for help, there had been no sign of rescue. And now, they were going to die here, in the dark, one by one, leaving no memory of themselves behind to be mourned.

The farm back home had been a grand celebration of life each and every day as they fed on only the greenest pastures and most delicious grains, trotting and grazing about the land that flowed with milk and honey. At the ranch, the word "tomorrow" always held a promise of sunshine, flowers, and frolicking to their hearts' content. Their owner had loved them dearly, giving them only the sincerest of care. Oh how they missed his reassuring voice calling out each day as the sun rose over the hill! Not a word from his call was ever understood by the likes of them, but his tone, his sweetness, his sensitivity and thoughtfulness…all that was communicated above any natural barriers. He spoke the language of humans, but he whispered the language of the animals. The sheep, cows, goats, dogs, cats, chickens, mules, and horses all knew by their owner's smile and gentle touch that they were loved.

Then one day, without warning, he stopped coming to the barn.

"Ready?" Nita adjusted herself into a "crisscross-applesauce" position on the bed, waiting patiently for her younger sister's response.

"Yep! Let's play."

For the first several days, the farm animals remained puzzled by their owner's absence. The optimistic horses believed he would return, but the rest of them were not convinced. Their bellies were growling in demand for the farmer's usual banquet, and their hearts longed for his jovial banter, but alas, as the hours stretched without his singsong arrival and the rustling of grain bags, their morale dipped to a breaking point. Not a sound had been heard from the farmhouse. Not a movement had been seen in his windows. Not a single vehicle had driven up the long driveway to visit.

Food supplies were quickly dwindling. The animals had no choice but to leave their home and travel as a group elsewhere in search of the life-giving sustenance the mysteriously-disappeared farmer had always provided.

Althia bent over the gathered animals and removed the plastic hay bales, removing them completely from the scene. "Nita, help me move this green blanket so the animals don't have any more grass to eat."

"Oh, good idea!" Nita said.

When the blanket was removed, they continued.

A plan was developed, voted on, and set in motion. Lightning and Rosie, a white horse and a pink pig—the inseparable leaders of the barn when the farmer was away—would stay behind in case the farmer reappeared. Lightning always had a way of communicating trouble to his master, and no doubt the farmer would saddle up and ride Lightning to catch up with the others if it came to that. The rest of the farm animals would leave at dawn.

As the sun once again rose beautifully over the rolling hills of the land-scape, the animals set out. The sky was blue and vibrant. The air was perfect for the journey. All melancholy thoughts were temporarily replaced by gratefulness that in spite of their sad departure from all things familiar, the weather was in their favor for the voyage. But this newfound determination would not last.

When the harsh and unexpected hailstorm came a couple of hours later, floods rose in the valleys as small fragments of ice tore into their fragile hooves and talons, forcing them to climb the steep incline toward a protective cleft in the mountainside.

"Wanna use this cup for the cave?" Nita asked.

"No, it's too small. They won't all fit." Althia glanced about for a moment, and then grabbed a shoebox. Layering the gray blanket inside, she tilted the shoebox for their makeshift cave.

It was there, on that very outcrop, that they discovered the perfect shelter to stay huddled together inside until the sun once again dominated the sky.

But it was there, in that very cave, that they would perish, if help did not arrive…

Darkness was coming soon, and with it the cruel frost. They didn't stand a chance of surviving even one more night in the bitter cold without food. By now, most of them were lying on their sides, eyes closed, faith lost, anticipating the same outcome tonight as all the rest.

A bright blue goat hushed the others and stepped forward as she had done every single day since the avalanche had entrapped her and her friends in the fissure of the mountain's edge weeks before. One neon yellow pig oinked in protest of her insistence that she had, once again, heard something in the distance.

The rest of the animals didn't even flinch while the goat stepped her rigid, plastic hooves dangerously close to the cliff's dropping point.

Nita observed this daring move, and eyed Althia with caution.

"Don't worry," Althia said, observing her older sister's expression. "I know what I'm doing. She won't fall. The blue one is my favorite."

"Okay."

"You guys hear that?" the blue goat asked.

Nobody answered.

"You guys hear that?" she asked again.

Still, nobody answered. Ever the optimist, this goat had given them false hope one too many times since the avalanche. Not one of them believed that this sound she thought she heard would be any different. One sea-green horse huffed in annoyance. A canary-yellow chicken ruffled her feathers. Several long moments transpired and the persistent goat leaned ever farther into the dangerous open air.

"Guys, it's for reals this time! You hear that?"

"I do…" said a voice a few feet behind her.

When the old, faithful, purple barn cat whipped his head up suddenly and turned his attention to the cave's opening, the animals froze. If any among them had the better hearing, as well as the night vision required to see farther than a few feet from their perch in the relentless invisibility of twilight, it would be a feline.

"Why does the cat always have to be the smart one?"

"Because," Nita answered, "cats can see really far when it's getting dark, and they have really good ears."

"But the blue goat was gonna be the first to hear it this time," Althia stated, a concerned pout materializing.

"Wait, I know! Let's pretend they do it together."

"Okay!"

Satisfied once again with the joint effort, Althia smiled and moved the blue goat a little to the left to allow room for Nita's purple cat to join her in the coming revelation.

The horses held their breath. The sheep turned their ears. The mule in the back silenced himself mid-heehaw.

Silently, the purple barn cat leapt over the backs of the other animals with graceful agility and focused his eyes fiercely out into the countryside. Although there was no trace of movement as far as he could see, his posture stiffened and his ears perked.

There was definitely a sound in the distance, and it was getting closer. But it wasn't the sound in itself that immediately inspired terror.

It was the rhythm.

They would know that gallop anywhere…

"Hey," Nita said, suddenly turning her head about the floor. "Where's Thunder?"

"You're sitting on him," Althia answered with a laugh.

"Oh!" Nita giggled, grabbing a black horse out from below her thigh.

Instantly, the sounds continued from Nita's mouth, a low, growly, villainous "clippity clop" mirrored by her angry facial expression. Her hand jabbed Thunder against the blanket repeatedly in sharp, fuming galloping motions. "Those farm animals can't have *my* cave!" she voiced.

Finally, the silence among the farm animals was broken. Shuffling, scraping, and hoof trots erupted and echoed off the cavernous walls as the farm animals crowded together, all straining their eyes and ears out into the encroaching night.

"Oh no," the cat said. "It's him. It's Thunder!"

There on the ground below them was a beastly stallion, black as the void, eyes fixed on the farm animals forbiddingly. Thunder threw back his head, reared up on his hind legs, and released a terrifying, screeching neigh into the sky. The sky responded with a rolling torrent of furious rumbling, a thunderous roar that penetrated the animals' bones to the marrow.

The sight was menacing, chilling...bloodcurdling. Fear gripped the animals as they backed away, only the purple cat and the blue goat showing the bravery to face their nemesis.

"You have no power here, Thunder," the goat said. "Go away! We were here first! You are the personification of sin!"

Nita struggled to hide her smirk at her sister's chosen words. The "personification of sin" was a string of words they had heard on television earlier that day. It was likely that Althia had waited all day to deliver this line in character, and it was just as likely that she didn't have a clue what the words even meant, but they sounded like something that would describe the bad guy, and Nita was determined not to steal Althia's moment by poking fun.

"Dinner!" a voice shouted from the back room.

Althia and Nita both deflated.

"Oh man, we just got started! Thunder just came into the story!" Althia slumped and crossed her arms.

Nita sat thoughtfully for a moment. "Here, let's just finish real fast, and then we can start a new one after we eat."

Althia considered this option with visual protest. Knowing, however, that there was no other option but to pause the game at the moment

Thunder had threatened the safety of the animals—*which was not an option*—she nodded reluctantly, glanced at the bedroom door, and then moved to a position on her belly, propping her chin on her hand, ready to rush the ending with intensity and fervor.

Suddenly, without warning, another sound was heard off in the distance, interrupting the exchange. This time, everyone heard it. The heroic pounding of Lightning's hooves—striking the ground, tearing into the earth, splashing puddles, propelling forward, closer and closer—inspired hope within the hearts of the fear-stricken and abandoned animals. The blue goat and the purple cat looked everywhere, frantically, but the source of the sound was out of sight.

The other animals each in turn responded with growing trepidation. Thunder had appeared, planning to lay claim on—

"Dinner's ready. Come and eat. Food's gettin' cold!"

This time the voice was just outside the door, accompanied by an impatient knock.

"Aw, man! Coming, Mom!" Althia whined.

"Hurry, hurry." Nita advanced Lightning's far-off position from over the pillowy hills and brought him to stand within sight of the cave. She leaned over, grabbed Rosie, and crammed her down onto Lightning's back in a riding position.

Replicas of Lightning and Rosie, the plastic toys that filled our dreams and adventures.

That was how Lightning and Rosie usually traveled.

"Wait! Wait!" Althia said frantically. Pulling one of the earlier-retired plastic hay bales from the bag, she awkwardly shoved it, also, onto Lightning's back, held just barely secure between Rosie's front feet. "Rosie has to bring the food."

"Oh, yeah."

And then, just in front of a billowing whirlwind of dust at the foot of a remote hill, appeared Lightning, in all his perfect, white, plastic splendor. On his back, like the magnificent benefactor that she had always been, was Rosie, the faithful pink pig, balancing on her hind legs, and carrying enough food in her front trotters for all the previous farm inhabitants. This brought the following triumphant trumpeting from an otherwise silent cave. Every horse, every pig, every chicken, goat, cow, cat, and dog found a voice in that instant, from the tiniest bleat to the loudest heehaw.

"It's Lightning and Rosie!" the blue goat announced. "We're saved! And Rosie brought food! Just you wait, stupid Thunder! Lightning's gonna—"

"Althia! Nita! Dinner! Now!"

The patience had gone from Mom's voice. Time was up.

"Okay," Nita said, assuming her position as older sister and, therefore, leader of the game. "Let's just pretend that they fought and Lightning wins. We're gonna get in trouble."

"But I don't just want to leave the farm animals in the cave like this."

"I know. Me either. But Mom's gonna get mad."

Althia sighed, rose up from the mattress, and headed out of the bedroom door without another word.

Nita followed suit.

A moment later, the bedroom door opened again. Nita ran quickly to the bed and flicked Thunder with the tip of her middle finger. The small toy went soaring across the scene and toppling to its demise under the edge of the tilted shoebox.

"That's better," Nita said with a smile, turning a final time toward the evening meal. The story may have only just begun when it was derailed with Mom's dinner plans, but Nita knew she wouldn't be able to enjoy her meal if the animals had been abandoned without care and in close proximity to Thunder. Their safety had to be—*always had to be*—ensured before the game could be stopped.

✤

Imagination. Reality in the mind of a child… When the real world just isn't enough.

Some folks remember escorting the maiden out of danger, defeating the fire-breathing dragon of the attic, and saving the kingdom of the living room. Others recall the time they fought back the beast of the garage with a sword, leading a victory march with the neighborhood kids through the backyard and into blessed freedom.

The world adults live in is boring and underwhelming a great deal of the time when compared to the adventures brewing within a child's mind. Children play because they can escape mundane reality and not feel silly or embarrassed doing so. Yet what many adults overlook when observing little people at play is that the scenario they choose to plot out often speaks of that child's character and passions.

This does not suggest that a kiddie game will be an indicator of life outcome, however. A child chosen in a group to be the bad guy may grow up to be the sweetest humanitarian the world has ever known. A little girl merely playing as the sidekick or support to the heroine out of shyness may blossom into the next world leader. A young one who reverts to the casual "playing house" may cast the simple, all-American family life aside in later years in trade for an adventurous career. But as any child psychologist will tell you, playtime is an opportunity to "try on" different personalities, shapes, molds, and ideas, harmlessly toying around with new concepts of our identity. Although it's obvious that no one is defined by what his or her imagination brings to life in youth, it is in those precious early moments that, if a parent or guardian is observing well enough, some of the biggest tell-tale signs of inner potential reveal themselves.

My sister and I had many great adventures. It is true that we almost never deviated from our favorite games, but within those games uncountable plots unfolded.

We had but few props: a bed, stuffed animals, and one eighty-eight-cent bag of tiny, plastic, rainbow-colored farm animals.

Lightning was a white horse, Rosie was a pink pig, and Thunder—the enemy and bully of all the other animals—was a black horse. These, along with the other colorful animals, came from the eighty-eight-cent farm animal grab-bag. The story was always different, but many times it included similar themes: the animals were abandoned with no food, ended up stranded, and Lightning would faithfully run to their rescue just in the nick of time, with "good ol' Rosie" on his back, holding enough food to feed all the other animals during their plight. The two of them together saw that every animal was saved. At some point in every story, Thunder would show up to further threaten the farm animals in the most conniving ways the minds of five- and six-year-olds could conceive. He and Lightning had many brutal fights.

Over and over again, Lightning proved the victor with his pudgy, pink sidekick.

Our family moved a great number of times throughout my childhood. As a little girl, it felt like every day was a new house, a new school, new peers, and new shuffling about in our daily lives. I was always the awkward new kid, and just when I had started to grasp on to what a school or culture had been teaching me, I was whisked away from all familiarity and introduced to a different community with the latest expectations of my behavior, education, dress, social skills, and overall human performance. We rarely had enough time to connect with the world around us before it swirled and blurred out of focus and into new—and once again foreign—surroundings. With little ability and opportunity to form lasting relationships with anyone outside the home, and since my brothers were older and held different interests, Althia was my rock. My constant. Each time we relocated, the dreaded announcement was made that we would have to leave some things behind for lack of space. The two of us would scramble to shove every single precious toy into any crevice we could find, including the bottoms of our brothers' moving boxes, between (and under) the seats in the car, or inconspicuously wedged into the middle of blankets and towels…any place where a toy could be concealed, because my dad had told us we could keep whatever we could fit into the truck. However, regrettably, during each move, Althia and I still parted with some of our dear stuffed "friends" we had so earnestly cared for together. Lightning, Rosie, Thunder, and the others were among the elite. Nothing could tear those gems loose from my grasp, no matter how many times we moved.

And, as I began to understand in my later years, there was a significant reason for this.

One of my husband's most recent books, *Redeemed Unredeemable: When America's Most Notorious Criminals Came Face to Face with God* (also including Donna Howell as coauthor), included a chapter on the

1980s controversial parent-killer, Sean Sellers. His earliest and most crucial years of social development were immersed in constant displacement, paving the way for a deep disconnect within his concepts of the value of human life. This, as the reader discovers in the book, played a major role in shaping his initial mold. He moved to new homes continuously, frequently placed in the care of temporary guardians while his parents were traveling. As an only child, he was never able to make or maintain friendships, and endured abuse in places many other children would find safety. Over time, his worldview became an inward one. Since the only friend he could keep was himself, he, *himself,* became the only friend he cared about. Although these circumstances certainly do not excuse the murders he later committed, this case study on his life canvases what a person filled with extreme intelligence and potential can become when subjected to instability of such magnitude during childhood development: a warped, demented shape far, *far* from what God would have intended for such a life.

Unlike Sean Sellers, I had Althia.

Along with Althia, we had Lightning and Rosie.

Parting with them was out of the question.

And what they stood for, in both of us, was *real.*

In his album, *The Champion,* popular Christian music artist Carmen performed a song called "The Destination Is There." The words of the chorus have profound meaning:

Your desire is the confirmation, the destination is there.
God wouldn't put it in your spirit, if it wasn't going nowhere.
So, set your sights on the promises and don't you be scared.
Cuz your desire is the confirmation; the destination is there.

(Chorus from: Carmen, "The Destination Is There," *The Champion*, performed by Carmen, produced by Keith Thomas and Lynn Nichols, Word Records, 1985.)

Each time I buckled myself into the car destined for a new place, looking over my shoulder as yet another of our homes shrank in the distance and into the past, it had never occurred to me who or what I was being shaped into. Like many children, I had entertained thoughts of what I would be "when I grow up." But, like many children, I couldn't have possibly wrapped my brain around how the circumstances of my life were molding me during those moments.

The desire in my heart sang "pony, pony, pony!" The thoughts in my head rang "horsies, gallop, whinny!" But along with such happy, fantasy-inspired dreams, there was a little girl who was lost on the inside. My mold was spinning and jerking me left and right—matched only by the confusion of my ever-changing surroundings—grasping for a stability that could never be found as long as my sights were on settling into a permanent home and reaching out to people my own age. I wasn't anywhere near old enough to articulate the hole I felt growing inside as a result of my need to connect with the world in a healthy way, but it was present, and it was dramatic, an unseen force pulling my confidence and beliefs of my own potential into a whirlwind.

Imagine my surprise last year when I read the case study on Sean Sellers' life. Although there were many things we did not have in common, I understood all too personally how a child in a constant state of travel and relocation could struggle with social attachment. But my greatest moment of shock in his chapter was when I realized I had moved even more times in my childhood than he did...

But the desire was my confirmation.

The destination was there.

What would I become?

As an adult, I have reflected on the characters of Althia and my favorite games. Lightning was a hero. A protector of animalkind. A dominant guardian. No bully like Thunder would have the last laugh while Lightning was around. No single animal would be left behind. All inhabitants of the farm were equally important to Lightning—from the blue goat to the purple barn cat. Rosie was the nurturer. Every animal would receive the care it deserved, not by earning that care with good works, but simply by being a farm animal and, therefore, an equal amidst its peers. Thunder was the opposition. His presence shook the stability and safety of the animals at crucial moments in the stories we plotted. When the animals already had so many fears, abandoned, cold, hungry, and lost, Thunder was always the final confrontation. The ultimate conflict. The keeper of the keys to happiness and rescue.

And the farm owner? He never came back in the story…

Not once.

I am not a psychologist, but if I were to analyze what these characters stood for in my young psyche, I would assume that the farm owner was the embodiment of instability, the whirlwind of circumstances unknown, the entity that never saw to return things to normal and bring safety and assurance. Lightning saved the animals not only from the wreckage of whatever situation the plot had put them in, but from their loneliness and friendless surroundings, putting the protection of his own family above all else. Thunder represented the thing these animals had to be protected *from*, the social force to be reckoned with when things felt they couldn't get any worse, the stranger that represented a disconnect or unhealthy association to peer relations. Rosie provided for the animals' needs like a missionary to a desolate land, tossing out items for the needy to outstretched hooves like the reformed Ebenezer Scrooge the first Christmas morning after his ghostly visitations.

As Althia and I played out our silly games, it wasn't anywhere near that complicated. We did not develop intricate, psychological storylines that sought to mend broken hearts or minister to souls with an eternal focus. We were just rescuing rainbow animals, beating the bad guys, and ushering in the idyllic "happily ever after" time and time again. Standard-issue kiddie play. We were choosing our own roles rather than the roles dictated to us by a never-ending list of adults in our ever-changing communities that we would never know long enough to conform to or please. But somewhere down deep, as Lightning and Rosie were saving the day, I was processing my own reality, viewing the puzzle pieces of my whirlwind life, working out the edges, and purging instability from the inside out. Lightning and Rosie were my lifeline, the only things over which I truly held ownership.

Someday, years later, after some space and time had been given for me to view these pieces from a greater distance, I would see that my first horse-related lesson had been taught.

It wasn't just what Lightning was to the animals, it was what *I wanted to be*. It was the desire of my heart. A rescuer. A protector. A mentor. The relief from pain and suffering. The rescue party. The salve to festering wounds upon those who were lost in their own dark and abandoned caves. The friend to those who had been abused and tormented by their own bullies, their own Thunders.

And the desire of my heart, as I would learn later on, was my confirmation that the destination was there from the beginning…from the womb (Jeremiah 1:5). God would not have put that in my spirit if He hadn't the plans to carry it on to completion (Philippians 1:6). And I, that awkward little girl in used clothing with an eighty-eight-cent bag of plastic farm animals, had been chosen from before the creation of the world to be used in love toward others in the unique ways He had instilled within me (Ephesians 1:4).

Interestingly, this lesson was deepened by another favorite game during that time. Our bed, or "flying carpet," was the vehicle in which Althia and I would bring our mobile medical veterinary assistance to the most broken of all our stuffed collections. As we soared high above the earth among the clouds, relaxing in the crisp breeze, the momentum of our enchanting flight emanated, a wounded animal would be spotted. Immediately, our flying carpet would be navigated to the ground and our surgical rescue would commence. I was the surgeon; Althia was the nurse. A rip in the seams of a brown teddy bear, a missing eye from a red fox, a cotton stuffing hemorrhage from the belly of a purple horse…all wounded animals were an opportunity.

As we were always moving to new homes and communities, and with little financial means to support toy hobbies, many of the stuffed animals my sister and I owned were obtained through thrift shops, yard sales, or hand-me-downs. Thus, many of the toys we had were broken from the start. And when allowed to peruse the toy aisles of second-hand stores with a quarter or two to spend, we often specifically sought after imperfection. Many children with limited means may settle for what they can afford, but would, if given the option, choose newer, prettier toys to decorate their living spaces.

Not me. And not Althia.

The worse off the toy, the more preciously it fit into our agenda to bring them healing and restoration.

As the flying carpet would come aground, I leapt from my perch and hurried to the mortally injured animal. Althia would hold the animal down and assist me with my tools while I completed the surgery. With a needle and thread, we sewed these animals back together, patching and restoring them to full health. Over and over and over.

One may wonder why we frequently had toys that needed mending. Sometimes our older brothers, being the *boys* that they were, would come into our room when nobody was looking and kidnap our furry friends for use in a pillow fight, throw them against the wall, or rip them up and toss them all over the room just to get a rile out of us girls. Initially, it angered us greatly. Mom always tried to keep them from doing this, but she always had a lot of other things to do. If she turned her head for a second, the boys were up to something, and our stuffed toys were frequently the victims of these mischievous moments. But, after the fury had subsided, we would fire up the flying carpet and zoom through the clouds once more, inevitably restoring these critters via our charitable medical services.

To many, a broken toy is a worthless object, an unpleasant thing to look at, an item to skip over and avoid. To me, it was valued, loved, treasured, and *restored*.

In one of Jesus' most incredible and memorable parables, a man was accosted by robbers on the road between Jerusalem and Jericho. They beat him nearly to death, stole his clothes, and left him stranded. A priest happened by the injured man and ignored him, choosing to travel the opposite side of the road. Soon, another man from the tribe of Levi saw the victim as well. He, too, continued on the opposite side of the road. It wasn't until the third man, the Good Samaritan, came upon the man bleeding, naked, and alone, that true value was seen in a life so otherwise deemed inconvenient. Not only did this Samaritan stop his travels to dress the man's wounds, he placed the man on his own donkey and took him to an inn where he continued to care for him. In the morning when his duties required him to be elsewhere, the Samaritan brought forth coins from his own purse, paying the innkeeper to look after the man and promising that he would return later to check on the patient and reimburse the innkeeper for any further costs.

After Jesus told his parable of the Good Samaritan, He asked His listener who of the three strangers on the road to Jericho was "neighbor" to the man lying helpless on the road. When the listener answered that it had been "he that shewed mercy," Jesus responded, "Go, and do thou likewise" (Luke 10:29–37).

Jews and Samaritans: natural enemies. Yet this did not stop the good man from helping the friendless.

I had not heard this story until years following our own little "Good Samaritan" game. My sister and I had no motive to play parallel to the Scriptures we had not yet heard. We were not driven by a moral code that we had adopted from a church we had never attended. The desire of our hearts was not learned, but innate.

I am not intending in this contrast to elevate myself as a saint above anyone else, and especially not above a child who prefers pretty toys. I am a grandparent now, and at every birthday and Christmas, I shower my grandkids with brand-new items, still in the packaging. In truth, I was a typical scraggly kid with my own ornery moments, like anyone. The purpose of this reflection is not to impress anyone with depictions of little-Nita grandeur, but to share an amusing association. I can't help but think how many others discarded these toys because they had already served their purpose in their glory days. They were ugly. They were useless. Broken. Inconvenient. The horse with stuffing falling from his stomach in the free box at the garage sale had likely been passed over so many times, its value in question because of the condition it was in.

Who would want a broken or damaged toy? Nobody should or could be blamed for refusing to invest in such a material thing.

But to me and my sister, these toys were among those that *most* needed a home. They were those that needed love, care, and companionship so much more than all the others, and to provide that was *our* honor. An honor we shared.

Without knowing it at the time, we were being led—and I believe by God—to put the principle of the Good Samaritan into practice. No stuffed animal, no plastic farm toy, would be left behind.

All had value.

All would be rescued from uncertainty and dilemma.

All would be brought into the arms of safety and stability.

When Carmen wrote the words, "Your desire is the confirmation, the destination is there," he touched on something that is true for every soul under God. We may not understand the desires of our heart before they are carried to fruition, and we may at times question whether these desires have anything to do with ministry opportunity or even eternity. But the desire is confirmation that someday you will arrive at the destination God placed on your life journey map while you were still in the womb. Carmen understood that. So much so, that when the aforementioned parent-killer Sean Sellers was in prison on death row, awaiting execution, Carmen met with him personally as a mentor and personal pastor, counseling him until the end. As Sellers lay on his execution gurney, facing death, Carmen was eight feet away, praying for this young life. (See: Thomas Horn and Donna Howell, *Redeemed Unredeemable: When America's Most Notorious Criminals Came Face to Face with God* [Crane, MO: Defender Publishing, 2014], 168–171.) Not even with a death sentence did Carmen, this Good Samaritan, believe a single soul like Sellers could be discarded or left behind on his own travels to Jericho.

If Carmen was right—and I believe that he was—then He who began a good work in you will be faithful to complete it.

God's leadings within you are usually in harmony with who He made you to be, assuming the desires of your heart are pure. You are wired on the inside like a machine ever inching toward a goal that will bring happiness to you as well as to your Creator. Do not fall into the trap that assumes that anything personally gratifying or rewarding could not be God's will. Why would He create you with these inclinations and then expect you to pursue unrelated avenues? Certainly, paths unrelated to your passions will cross with the one you wish to travel, and these are the moments that will stretch you, place you in the heat for tempering, creating a more flexible mold, but this does not mean we were not given desires that match our gifts as they relate to His purposes.

After all, He made us in the first place.

Your talents and interests are driving you.

What's *your* destination?

2

Coco

*F*or as long as she could remember, Nita had wanted a horse. This unending, overwhelming obsession tore at her heartstrings constantly.

Other children wanted ponies, too. It seemed to be a traditional and universal fantasy for every little girl: the white, gentle, hypnotizing steed with a long, flowing, silver mane and tail, always catching the light just right as it appears among the backyard greenery, ready to carry its rider away on a saddle of gold toward a lifetime of adventure and camaraderie.

The difference between her longing for a horse and others' was that Nita knew well enough to visualize horses as they *were*: imperfect personalities requiring much food, maintenance, and training, and whose appearance was just as enduring in real life, when their coats were muddy from rolling in the grass and cockleburs created huge tangles in their hair.

It wouldn't matter what the horse looked like, or what personality it had. It didn't make any difference if it fit the depiction of a fantasy. Nita wanted a horse…*any* horse.

"Nita, are you listening?"

Nita snapped from her equestrian thoughts to stare up at her mother. "Um, yes. Sorry. I'll go see what Dad wants."

Nita and Althia had just started a game of Lightning and Rosie when Mom had called them to the kitchen. Dad had been outside for a few minutes calling for the kids, but they were so caught up in plotting the latest plight for the plastic farm animals that they hadn't heard him.

Trekking to the porch and waving off a few dogs, Nita and Althia met their dad and brothers at the car. The boys were inside fighting over Dad's leftover sandwich cookies, a generic version of Oreos that Mom included in his lunches every day. Sometimes Dad ate them, but often he would bring them home for the kids. This time, Althia and Nita were too late to lay any stakes on them.

"Yeah, Dad?" Althia asked, opening the door and wedging in between the boys.

"Where are we going?" Nita asked.

"I got a place I'monna take you kids to today." Dad turned the key in the ignition, and the old engine fired up, stirring the dust on the ground beneath. Putting the car in gear, Dad settled back in the driver's seat as they moved forward. "Come out to my friend's barn with me."

"Why are we going to a barn?" asked John, the older of the two boys.

"Got somethin' I wanna show ya."

This day had started like any other day. Oatmeal with butter and brown sugar for breakfast, off to another new school filled with unfamiliar faces, and back home to the smell of Mom's good home cooking alongside the sloppy greeting of thirteen dogs...

But this day would *end* in a dream.

☙❦

I remember the first equine pet I ever had. He was a Shetland pony by the name of Coco (as named by the owner), the same color as hot cocoa, but with a flaxen mane and tail. He was absolutely stunning to me, and not because he fit the standard concept of a fantasy, but because he was *mine*.

That day Dad drove us kids to his friend's barn was unreal. When we arrived there, I was immediately drawn into the ambiance of the enormous barn. A building that size might give off the impression from the outside that it is either abandoned or at the very least oversized, with many dormant areas about its interior, but that simply wasn't the case. Everywhere you looked, there was motion and activity. People were taking care of the animals, of which there was a variety, and it seemed that in every corner something was eating, receiving a brush-down, being corralled… It was a menagerie of life, and my mind was reeling by the implications that we might—just might—get to pet a pony or two.

Before long, a man emerged from within a stall with a small brown pony. I was in love with him immediately. At that moment I was convinced that just being allowed to touch him on the nose would put a spring in my step for a week. Just being near him and getting a close look at him was a bigger thrill than any I had felt for a long while. Dad asked if we liked him. I don't remember how the others in my family responded. I honestly don't remember my own response, either. I simply recall animatedly launching into all the ways I loved him.

There was no way I could have prepared myself for what happened next. It was a rushed blur of emotion so intense that the memory of my excitement cancels out my memory of the minute details of how Coco eventually ended up on our land. But Dad agreed we could keep him, and my eight-year-old heart exploded into a rapturous joy to which all other moments of happiness in my life to follow would be compared.

He was beautiful to me. I mean really, *really* beautiful. For days after his arrival, I had the hardest time functioning in my normal life. Chores, school, sleep, meals in the home—all of these routines were of great burden. When I was in Coco's presence, I was immersed in euphoric feelings of adoration for everything he was and everything he did, from the tiniest ear flick to the swishing of his tail. When he wasn't nearby, my thoughts wandered uncontrollably to the point that I was useless in any task until I could return to him. And when chores were done, school was over, and I wasn't needed at the house, butterflies erupted in my stomach as I drove my legs as hard as I could to find and visit my newest friend.

I was absolutely star struck.

For a time, all obstacles in my life were muted. Brothers picking on me, discomfort at school, feelings of social awkwardness, and all other drama lifted its sting as I knew I had a cocoa-brown pony friend waiting for me at home to ride with the wind. Technically, Coco belonged to all of us equally, but I defied anyone to say that he wasn't *my* pony. I spent more time with him than anyone, and he responded more to my presence than the others. It truly was, in every sense of the phrase, my dream come true.

I didn't even mind that Coco was a total stinker! In his mind, he was the owner and I was the servant. After about an hour of riding, he usually decided he'd had enough. It wasn't *just* that he would buck me off; certainly not. He had a favorite landing pad in mind for me when he was ready to free himself of the burden on his back, and just about the time I saw him heading for that sharp, prickly holly bush, I knew it was coming. Sure, I was annoyed each time I had to get up, brush the dirt off my legs, pick the holly leaves out of my shins, and nurse the cuts and scrapes from the fall, but at the end of the day, I didn't care. Coco was my trusty companion, and no cantankerous jaunts toward the thorns were going to make me love him any less. In fact, Althia and I took great joy in an idea I had, a way of outsmarting him at his own game. We would wrap ourselves in a sleeping bag before heading out, and his holly-bush charges became more of a fun game than anything. We would merely get up and laugh after the tumble. (Don't ask me how we managed to straddle the pony's back with a sleeping bag on. Althia and I were both small, as was Coco, so somehow we made it work. It's just one of the many things kids do…)

My affection for him only grew when I realized Coco thought he was a dog.

Just down the highway from our house in Centralia, Washington, was a one-stop shopping store called "Yard Birds." A huge, black bird statue stood in the front. Inside, during that era, it operated much like a major shopping supercenter, comparable to today's Walmart. (Although the original Yard Birds buildings have largely been preserved from the outside, when last I visited around the year 2000, on the interior they were more of a flea-market-style consignment shop.) The pet section sold pet foods and livestock supplies. As a way to draw customers in to view their wares, the management agreed to take in just about any litter of puppies from anywhere and of any breed, and they gave them away for free. People would see the free puppies in the window and flock to pet them, which often led to an impulsive puppy adoption, along with the purchase of new supplies for the happy pet owner. Not only did this financially benefit the store, it was outlet way for anyone in the community to pass on the responsibility of a fresh litter to someone reliable. As a result, Yard Birds quickly became the community go-to for puppies and pet supplies, and for many in the local area, visiting that store was more than just a shopping trip, it was an event.

For my mother, it was torture.

Dad would visit the store for dog food, but without fail, when his truck came up the driveway, he would emerge with both the food and yet another dog. At any given time, we had eight, ten, twelve, even thirteen dogs all running free around our property. Mom was always bummed to see this. I remember hearing her more than once moan, "Oh, now, come on... Not another dog!"

Needless to say, it was understandable that Coco fancied himself a canine.

Since the use of food bowls had long since been dismissed as a trivial nuisance in view of so many competing mouths, Mom would grab the dog food, head to the yard, and dump the chow directly onto the ground. Her mealtime summon to the dogs reflected her Oklahoma farm upbringing as she shouted the hog call, "Sooieee, sooieee!" Like a panting, slobbery, motley band of clumsy wild animals, they stampeded toward the house to jockey for food as if every meal was their last. Dogs would appear from all over the property: behind the barn, out in the fields, under the cars, under the porch... Every direction you turned, tripping dogs appeared bounding over rocks and dirt mounds, hurtling over each other, barking like mad, tumbling about in the pursuit of kibble.

And then, from the back of the group, Coco would gallop directly into the fray, kicking the dogs to the side, rearing his head against their ribcages, knocking the challengers out of the race like a bowling ball to the pins. Once at the food, his hind end was evermore poised toward his canine brothers, vying to establish his dominant position at the feast.

With all the grass he could wish for, ripe at all times, and more nutritionally appropriate for a pony on any given day, rivaling Coco still had something to prove.

Coco was the alpha dog.

But dog food was *not* the only bizarre fare Coco had added to his own personal banquet. Evidently, he also thought he was human.

Dad was a smoker. He typically kept his cigarette pack in the front pocket of his shirt. Crazy Coco had mastered the art of snatching Dad's smokes right out of the package—and right in front of Dad's face— faster than Dad could react. In one fell swoop, the cigarettes were there one second and gone the next. Coco loved his tobacco. Even Dad's beer was up for grabs if Coco was around. He would nab and run off with nearly anything—ice cream, soda, a sandwich—from the hand of an unsuspecting man, woman, or child. Though Dad quickly caught on to Coco's shirt-pilfering tactics, Dad's sandwich cookies were never safe while the windows of the truck were rolled down.

And sleep? There would be no stall bed for *this* ridiculous pony.

One of my brothers, risky as they often were, had once caught a mattress on fire. Mom had made short work of the threat by dragging the mattress out of the bedroom window and onto the ground outside, where she proceeded to hose it down. It was left there right where it had landed, and remained deserted. But our trash became Coco's davenport. For hours on end, Coco would lie on his side, basking in the sun on his very own bed…and he wouldn't share. The various breeds of hounds would have to find their own treasure spot if he was anywhere near his resting place when they came around.

The pony was basically nuts.

But as history will tell, some of the greatest lessons have been learned from people and animals that fit the description of "nuts." One of my all-time favorites belonging to this category was the beloved actor Jerry Lewis.

Lewis is most remembered for his slapstick comedy in Hollywood films, always portraying the nerd, the klutz, or the fool. And although his roles were always masterfully executed, involving humorous spills, exaggerated falls, catastrophic accidents, and jerky awkwardness from an all-thumbs buffoon, nobody would deny that despite the clever delivery of his ungainly movie characters, he was also an incredibly talented performer. Many other actors and actresses of Hollywood during his time could dance with perfect timing, each step or tap in a choreographed number carried out with crisp precision. Lewis proved on many occasions in his films that he, also, harbored this same level of talent, beginning, carrying, and ending a song meticulously. However, for the sake of comedic flare, sometimes during an otherwise flawless dance routine, he would get just ahead of, or behind, the beat, flinging about the stage or movie set like a bungling dolt.

The commemorative DVD editions of Lewis' films often feature interviews with the actors or actresses who were cast to dance with Lewis. The challenge, these performers have said, was never about having the correct timing during a dance. (Generally, anyone chosen to play such a part would have already established that he or she had excellent musical timing, or the performer would not have been cast in the first place.) Rather, being forced by a character role to dance slightly *off time*, or holding to the correct timing while Lewis was off—*that* was the challenge.

I understand this very well. I have been a drummer for many years, and for many different styles of music. Playing the drums on the beat is a *must* for me. When I hear a band performing a song live and the drummer is skipping about the tempo like a metronome with a mind of its own, I can't help but react similarly to a vocalist hearing someone else singing off-key. It's uncomfortable. Unnatural. To someone who has perfect timing on the inside, and who has spent long hours developing the skills required to play the drums accurately, playing off-beat is by far more taxing than playing the right way. But when it can be done intentionally for the sake of a specific parodic performance, it's brilliant!

The viewers of Lewis' hilarity would agree.

The harder and more unexpected timing can once in a while be the most ideal, even when it's unpleasant or unnatural to the listener. It is a most ingenious paradox.

When my dad once again announced that we were moving to a new home, I wasn't surprised. By now, this had become our way of life. During the move, Dad boarded Coco with some friends "for just a few days." He took us to the place where Coco was boarded and we played with him for a few hours one day. I assumed we would get him back when we had unpacked our things. Sadly, though, that was not to be. Coco was a huge responsibility, and he needed land and accommodations we would not be able to provide at our new place. The people who had agreed to board him had expressed an interest in purchasing him as well, and Dad agreed, informing us all of the transaction later on.

I never saw Coco again.

It all happened so fast.

On one hand, I was devastated by the loss of my first pony. He was my friend, despite all his quirky behavior, and I knew then, and have always known since, that I would have loved that silly pony until the day he died. I would have given him the best care as any kid my age could have given. Everything he was to me was exactly as he had been: a very odd pet. I never sought to change him, and I appreciated him for a uniqueness apart from the little girl's cliché fantasy.

But, on the other hand, I knew from the beginning that our lifestyle did not support the ownership of such grand—and large—possessions. I guess you could say that I had seen it coming. Perhaps that is why I loved him as much as I did, because I knew deep down that our time together was limited.

I cried—*of course* I cried! When Dad told me Coco wasn't my pony anymore, it wasn't completely unexpected. It was life. Yet, that didn't make it any easier to say goodbye. Somewhere between the blow of not having a say in whether I would get to keep my favorite pet, and knowing that he had gone to a wonderful new home with owners equipped to care for him appropriately, I eventually accepted the fact that Coco was no longer mine, and that it was what was best for him.

Timing.

A virtuoso and inspired element of life. One that brings harsh dips and turns on the journey. Something you may never have control of.

Something *God* uses to shape the mold.

When I said my inner goodbye to Coco, I knew he wouldn't be my last equine friend. Now that I had finally owned a horse, now that my dream had at least for a time become a reality, I had proof that these elusive creatures were not only attainable and real, but that all along I had loved the real thing. Unlike many of my peers, I had somehow always known innately that these animals were more than just a ride into the sunset. When I connected with a genuine equestrian animal for the first time—not a *toy*—instead of finding that I was disappointed in what he really was, I learned that he, in all his individuality, was exactly what I wanted him to be. There had never been an anticlimactic moment in my experience of bonding with him. I had *tasted* it. But unfortunately, it was just a taste.

In the days following, I questioned the timing of his departure. I had been completely consumed with my dream of owning a horse or pony, and when I finally had been gifted with such a fortune, before I knew it, he was gone. In my young mind, I struggled with questions of whether that had been fair. Yes, it was our "way of life." And yes, it was "just how it goes sometimes." My ability to accept the otherwise unacceptable was no accident or coincidence. I had been well-tempered into this technique of understanding loss and giving up personal treasure for years before Coco had come along, and the day he arrived at my home, I knew it wouldn't last forever. *This*, however, had simply been too soon.

Looking back, I now know exactly what lesson was to be learned from Coco.

Like Jerry Lewis, Coco began his dance number in my life on cue. But the timing at the *end* of our dance was just as off-rhythm and unexpected as anything Lewis could have performed.

And, in reflecting on how that related to the rest of my future, the timing was brilliant. One could even say it was *ordained*.

I now knew that dreams could come true. Everything I had owned prior to Coco had been a toy, and now that I had tasted the real dish, I was only all the more determined that horses would play a significant role in my life yet to come. Coco had been an almost-dream, and he was the first of many almost-dreams that I would encounter.

Sometimes we feel teased by "preludes" of our heart's desires, and that can be discouraging on the surface. Yet, when our eyes are in focus on the experience the preludes bring, we can see that their purpose in our lives is as the appetizer for the main course. The "tease" is enough to keep us plugged into the ultimate vision, because without savoring a morsel of the dream, it may stagnate or fall away. Sometimes we are given just enough of what we want in order to keep us in the dance.

If it is in our hearts and it is in God's will, God allows the dream to be experienced while we are being heated and tempered toward the later goal. The heat is uncomfortable and the crackling sounds of the forge are frightening, but the end result is a stronger steel. God is the Maestro, the Conductor, the first and last Percussionist. It is to His drum—to His rhythm—that we should dance, always on the timing He ordains until the grand finale. But sometimes the sheer genius of the dance—the journey to the end result—is in the unanticipated and peculiar timing that it's delivered.

Many of us have at some point approached God like a fast-food drive-through. We tell Him what we want, and we are frustrated or confused when we don't get what we asked for. If we order a burger and fries, God might give us a healthy salad, instead. He knows what's best for us. We may not be given just the taste we're after, but it may just be the soul food He knows we need. Other times, we get to the second window of the journey after paying the price we feel was asked of us at the first window, just to hear God give us an unexpected update: "Not ready yet. Please pull forward and *wait*." We feel hungry for the main course *now*, but if the main course is served before it is fully seasoned and cooked, it won't satisfy our expectations, and the experience could be completely spoiled.

I had no idea I was going to be given Coco. When I had him, I loved him with the fullness of my heart, and it is clear to me now that God was allowing me to enjoy this gift while it could be enjoyed. When he departed from my life with hardly a goodbye, it was hard for me to know why, but at the least, my taste buds for the main course were whetted. But I had absolutely no idea that just around the corner, the biggest tragedy of my life would befall. Had we kept Coco, God only knows how complicated that relationship could have become.

3

The Pink Pony

*I*t was a standard, extended-stay motel at the edge of Glendale, Arizona, underwhelming to passersby from the road. Not by any means was it run down or shabby, but it was certainly not a Taj Mahal or Hilton either. It was a simple, family-budget location with minimal external attraction to catch the eye.

But for Nita, it promised adventure.

The horse-shaped sign read "The Pink Pony," and it sported a neon pink light that ran along the outline of a pony in mid-prance.

Nita certainly hadn't wanted to move again, and the sale of precious Coco was still fresh on her mind. But if they *just had to* relocate, at least they would be temporarily stationed in a motel dressed in an equestrian theme, as her father promised.

Nita rode along in the car with her mom, dad, and Althia as they drove past the Pink Pony motel. Her eyes danced about the outer walls of the building, drinking in the cacti that lined the twelve rental units on her left and her right, as well as the six in front. The air was hot, the sun was pouring down on the U-shaped structure, and the desert heat had long since stolen the luster of the pink paint on the doors. The tan color surrounding the doors had begun to chip, and the parking lot had never been paved.

Despite the nominal magnetism from the outside, however, Nita couldn't help but believe that any place with a name like "The Pink Pony" guaranteed nothing less than the ideal flight for the imagination. A castle in the sky. A mansion of splendor. An opulent and luxurious dwelling for her and Althia, as well as a blank canvas for the new developments of what was sure to be Lightning and Rosie's greatest episodes yet. Oh the wonders awaiting behind that locked door!

But it was not to be.

Unbeknownst to all of them, their stay at the Pink Pony motel would never come.

And by the time Nita would become informed of this, it would be the least of her worries.

✺

The biggest turning point in my story took place just after we kids were told we would be staying in the Pink Pony motel between houses. And as hard as it always is for me to revisit this nightmare, as difficult as it is for me to share this harsh reality with the world via this book that is otherwise filled with lightheartedness and laughter, my entire existence is largely defined by what happened next in my life. No autobiographical account of the lessons learned during my days on earth would be complete without the telling of the tragedy that occurred just after my thirteenth birthday.

My dad's father had recently passed away, leaving his vehicle to Dad. We were constantly on the move, and as a family of six with only one car, the need for another means of travel was no doubt a desperate one. We had been staying with my Aunt Juanita (who I am named after). The deposit to the Pink Pony had already been paid, and it was a matter of obtaining this additional car that stood between our temporary setting at Aunt Juanita's house and the extended-stay motel.

One night, after working outside, exposed in the desert sun and heat in a laborious setting all day, Dad came home and refreshed himself with a few cold beers. Between the exhaustion from work and the effect of the beer, he was completely out of it. It was that night Dad decided to load up and drive the fourteen-hundred-mile round trip to retrieve the car Grandpa had left him.

Althia didn't want to go. She begged to stay at Aunt Juanita's for what would have only been a four- to five-day trip to Modesto, California, and back. Mom and Dad allowed John and Terry, our older brothers, to stay behind, but she told Althia she had to ride along with the rest of us, a decision she would tragically come to regret for the rest of her earthly life.

As we were leaving on our journey, Dad stopped to buy us all an ice cream. Under normal circumstances I would have thoroughly enjoyed such a treat, but tonight something didn't feel right. There was a knot in the pit of my stomach. I didn't know if the ice cream was making me sick or if this odd sensation was coming from something else, but shortly after I dove into the icy delicacy, I remember looking out the back window of the car (as I had done so many times before while moving to a new location). I could still see the city lights shrinking as I tried to shake this odd sensation. I don't remember how it came that the ice cream was no longer in my hand, but before long, I was drifting to sleep. The seatbelt laws were different then, and we were not buckled in. As was typical during a long drive, my sister and I lay in a crisscross position, like a yin and yang overlapping, borrowing from the other's lap and body as a makeshift bed.

I don't know how long I slept before the jolt of the car woke me. I sat upright suddenly, and peered out the windshield. The desert road was dark and seemingly peaceful as we continued our drive. Mom was sleeping in the passenger's side front seat with her head against the window. Althia was asleep on my lap. All seemed well, and I was relieved that whatever had awakened me was evidently a negligible hiccup. A pothole, perhaps.

And then I noticed something a little out of the ordinary.

Dad continued to drive with his eyes forward, but his head bobbed limply, drowsily, as the car drifted into the sagebrush at the road's edge. The abrupt rattling of the car was enough to jerk him back to attention and veer back into the lane, but it lasted merely seconds before he was dozing off again.

Once he saw that I was awake, he engaged me in very unsettling conversation.

"Hey kiddo. Let's play a little game," he said.

"Um, okay," I responded timidly.

"Now you watch me. If you see the car going too far to the right, I want you to shout 'Left!' Okay? And if you see the car going too far to the left, I want you to say 'Go right!' Okay? Can you do that?"

I didn't like this game.

At thirteen years old, I couldn't find the words to explain why this felt so wrong to me. It was *Dad*. Clearly, he was the adult, and he knew what he was doing behind the wheel. As my parent, I was supposed to obey what he told me to do, and I usually did so without much protest.

This time would be no different, despite the apprehension growing in my gut.

After a few moments, Dad's head began to dip again, and the car approached the right edge of the road.

"Right!" I shouted. "No, left! *I mean left!*"

Dad's head popped back up and his hands directed the wheel quickly. A minute later, it happened again…and then again. This went on for a while as I sat, bewildered, terrible thoughts racing through my mind, but never lingering long enough for me to comprehend them, like a blur of unintelligible, buzzing chaos.

I have had years to reflect on that night, and I will never be able to put into words the suffocating feeling of foreboding that overtook me. Something bad was going to happen that night, *and I knew it*, but for reasons unknown even to myself, I felt powerless to stop it. The fear inside me was incredible. As Dad continued to float in and out of awareness, and as the wheels of our car coasted left and right sporadically, this feeling, this intense anxiety bubbling up in my body, rendered me useless to intervene. I sat there in my seat, hardly able to face the overwhelming and surreal circumstances I was observing. It was *more* than fear. It was an internal horror such as I had never before felt and have never felt since. A premonition of an end to which I couldn't fathom. An extrasensory perception that propelled me toward an act of silence that I will never understand. It was the most supernatural and indescribable dread I have ever felt.

Somehow, defying all attempts of explanation, my quavering and fright overpowered my ability to continue this game. I don't know if it stemmed from my wishing to escape such a forbidding sensation of imminent alarm, or if true physical exhaustion played a bigger role than

I have been able to assign it in my adult years, but in those moments of extreme panic, I eventually drifted back to sleep, setting the following event in motion.

I don't remember the crash. I just recall hearing sounds of shuffling and voices speaking about unfamiliar medical terms. When I opened my eyes, paramedics were strapping me to a gurney, preparing to lift me into an ambulance.

My left leg throbbed torturously.

The world was an incoherent blur.

I called out for Mom and Althia, but my cries were not answered. Without hesitation I began to wrestle against the gurney, straining to see what was going on around me and in an attempt to catch sight of my family. From what seems like everywhere all at once, the emergency responders fled toward me, telling me to remain still and calm down as others fixed a balloon splint to my leg. Their insistence that I relax angered me, and I responded to their warnings by thrashing about in a surge of adrenaline. From my mouth came the boldest gushing of profanities I have ever uttered. I cursed like a sailor, screaming demands that someone tell me the whereabouts of my mother and sister.

A few men surrounded me. It was likely a necessary sedation, but that scene cuts off from my memory as I drifted out of consciousness, coming to awareness again the moment I woke up in the hospital.

It had been a day since the accident.

Amidst foreign medical equipment in a bright, white, sterile room, came a man who introduced himself to me as "Dr. Arkunstein." It was too close to the name "Frankenstein" at that moment not to be crucially intimidating to my thirteen-year-old mind. Fear gripped me as the nightmare continued.

"Nita, I'm afraid I have some very bad news for you."

I didn't move. I merely stared at him blankly, expectantly, my heart pounding against my ribcage in angst.

"Last night, you and your family were involved in a terrible car accident."

This much I was aware of, but there was no preparing me for what I would hear next, and he wasted no time in delivering the blow.

"Your father didn't make it. He was killed instantly. Your mother is not doing so well. She has about a thirty percent chance of survival, and your sister has severe brain damage and we do not expect her to survive. However, if she does, she will most likely be a vegetable for the rest of her life."

Silence…

Shock…

The absence of life, itself…

Wake up!

Disbelief flooded my consciousness as the blood drained from my upper body. Althia, my best friend in the whole world, the only peer I have ever truly connected with, is not expected to survive? And if she does, she will be a vegetable? What does it mean to be a vegetable!? What was this strange medical speak this man was giving me, and why weren't they doing more to stop this from happening!? Hadn't medicine evolved to the point that these horrors only occurred in films? And why did Mom only have a *thirty percent chance*?

Although this man returned my unbelieving stare with sincerity and professionalism, the pity in his eyes for me clearly apparent, I could not help but feel that he was at that moment the cruelest and most vile enemy I had ever encountered. Like the ripping off of a Band-Aid, scab and all, he gave me what I'm sure he thought was the truth, and did so without batting an eye. This was unreal.

This *had* to be unreal.

I slapped my hands sharply against my arms in an attempt to jolt myself awake. I didn't want to keep having this disturbing dream.

Wake up!...

I did it again, and yet, I did not wake up.

I went numb. I was sure I had heard him incorrectly.

"No," I managed to say. "No... I wanna see my sister and my mom. Where's my mom?"

"She is in critical condition. So is your sister. There can be no visitors. I'm so sorry."

To be refused the chance to see the evidence of his words with my own eyes, I shook my head, rejecting the notion that it was not within my rights to immediately be brought before the two most important people in my life who, if this doctor was speaking the truth, needed my presence beside them now more than ever. The apology and concern lingering in his expression may have at any other point in life been soothing, but it served as only condescension after such harsh words as those he had spoken.

"*Let me* see my sister," I began firmly, my tone more resolved. "*Let me* see my mom."

"I am so sorry, but they cannot accept visitors right now," he explained again. "Your mother has suffered a puncture in both lungs and your sister has sustained severe head trauma. There is no way you can see them right now."

From deep within my spirit, from the depths of my very soul, I suddenly hated this vile man. He was the gatekeeper. The man who dared to exercise power and authority over my natural liberties as daughter and sister. There he stood, pretending to care about my welfare, all the while dangling the keys to reunion with my family like a steak to a starving wolf. Boiling within me, hot wrath gurgled and spat against all sensibility until an unrestrained abhorrence flowed. I completely lost control, becoming an unrecognizable monster, a mere shadow of the mild girl I had been. I screamed and kicked as much as my broken body would allow. I swore and hollered, ignoring the pangs and spasms my limbs offered in protest of my lashing out in explosive outrage.

"LET ME SEE MY SISTER! I WANNA SEE MY SISTER!" My jaw shuddered, sending a ruthless shooting pain through my neck as I screamed, but it was easy to ignore it in light of the demands that needed to be forcefully made.

His hands lifted and patted the air in an attempt to calm me. "I'm sorry, it's not possible," he said tranquilly. "Maybe in a day or so."

"TAKE ME TO MY SISTER! I WANNA SEE MY SISTER RIGHT NOW!"

This doctor couldn't possibly understand the emotional dynamics raging within me. I wouldn't understand them for years, either. My father had only seconds prior to this been removed from my life as any kind of potential safety figure, my sister and best friend was dying, and Mom was slipping. It was not out of callousness toward my father that I didn't speak of him then. Having been told that Dad was gone, my concern for him was lost in the haze of shock, of a reality my heart and brain refused to accept. A reality my heart and brain perhaps were incapable of accepting. All I could bring myself to think about was getting to those who were still alive, those who needed me, seeing them with my own eyes, and loving on them the way I knew I could if only I were just given the opportunity.

Maybe... Maybe in a day or so, he had said...

But my sister did not survive. Each day they promised to take me to see her, but they never did. I never saw her again after I kissed her goodnight in the car that night.

There are no words. Simply no words.

I was reduced to a shell of a person, anguishing in the purest of agony. I had lost my father. I had lost my sister. Based on the update I had been given, I was probably losing my mother. And I was in a neighboring state in a hospital where I knew no one.

Alone.

Miserably lonely days passed as I remained shell-shocked and internally defiant. This had to be some terrible joke the hospital staff had mercilessly played on me. It all felt real, and I knew that it was, but I kept hoping I would awaken from this nightmare to find my sister still asleep on my lap, Dad driving safely in the early light of dawn, and Mom's reassuring smile from the passenger's seat as we neared a rest stop for breakfast. I replayed those final moments over and over in my mind, hauntingly aware that although Dad was the driver, it had been *me* who dropped the ball on the game that may have kept everyone alive. How might the fate of my family been different had I intervened in some way?

I could have continued the left-right game.

I could have tried to convince my dad that he needed to stop for rest.

I could have roused my mom and insisted that she take the wheel.

I could have shaken my sister and engaged in horsie conversation to keep us both awake and alert to Dad's driving.

I could have…

I could have…

As the hours took their unsympathetic toll on my mind, body, and spirit, eventually the day came when my mother was stable enough to be moved from the small hospital in Needles, California. A retired Air Force pilot had volunteered his own small plane, as well as his time, money, and resources to a mercy flight in order to help relocate my mother and me to the Maricopa County hospital in Phoenix, Arizona, where we could be closer to my aunt Juanita and my brothers. From there, my then-deceased father and sister, who had been in the cargo compartment on the plane, were transported to a mortuary for the memorial service and burial (which we were unable to attend because we were still recovering at the county hospital).

As I was brought to the plane on my gurney for the mercy flight, I saw my mother for the first time since the accident. I had waited to reunite with a familiar face, and I so longed to see my pretty mom and hug her, feel her holding me, and rest in her reassurance, but the woman I saw was not the gentle, smiling, and welcoming woman I knew. She appeared as if she had been taken into a back alleyway and beaten with a baseball bat. Her body and face featured one continuing bruise from head to toe, purple and black spreading across her skin like a plague of death. Her condition was so alarming that I was amazed she was even alive. She looked as if she would pass away at any moment. The sight of my beautiful mother so badly beaten by the throw of the vehicle was like the final dagger into my emotional wall.

I got to her as quickly as the medical staff would carry me, but there would be no embrace. We merely grasped hands, and there, at the foot of the boarding bridge, on our gurneys, we finally loosed the tears that we had kept hidden until then.

I had never cried from emotional despair in the Needles hospital. I remember I had even tried to, because on some innate level I knew that tears would offer a release, as well as fulfill some kind of moral duty for someone who had just received the news that two loved ones had died. I can't say I completely understand it, except, perhaps, for shock, but I never cried about the news of my father and sister until I saw my marred and battered mother reaching for my hand. Once the dam broke, the tears flowed without restraint.

To this day, I often cry.

After we were released from the hospital, we began to piece together the details of the accident. Dad had fallen asleep at the wheel and crashed head-on into an oncoming diesel truck. My mother, my father, and I were the only people found at the scene. Had it not been for the cries from Mom and myself demanding to know where Althia was, the emergency responders may not have looked for my sister, who had been thrown so far from the car that she wasn't initially found. My father didn't suffer at all, as he had died instantly, and although my sister lived for a couple days with severe head trauma, I don't believe she suffered, either, because she never regained consciousness. Both of Mom's lungs were punctured and collapsed, and the bone in the lower half of her left eye socket was broken (later requiring plastic facial reconstruction surgery). I had suffered a broken leg, shattered jawbone, and cracked hip.

When news of our accident spread, kind-hearted people in Aunt Juanita's community placed little collection jars all over the city to help us with funeral expenses. The total funds collected were barely enough to pay for the burial, and as a result, Dad and Althia did not receive a headstone.

Mom and I both had our seasons of dealing with guilt and regret.

If I had only continued to play that silly right/left game…

If Mom had only allowed Althia to stay at Aunt Juanita's as she had begged to…

If only… If only…

As an adult, I no longer blame myself for the accident. Dad was at the wheel, and based on the game in the first place, I'm certain he knew he wasn't fit to be driving a car.

As the self-taught electrician previously employed by the Green Veneer Lumber Mill in Idanha, Oregon, Dad's work had integrated a huge wooden sign for the company that had been hung on the side of the building within view of all who came or left the facility, as well as from the highway. In white letters on a green background, the proud words "THINK SAFETY" served as a daily reminder to all at his company that he was watchful of hazardous activity while on the job. During the beginning of the development of what eventually became known as OSHA (Occupational Safety and Health Administration), state health and safety inspectors were arriving by the multitudes to many factory and occupational locations to enforce a higher standard of workplace protection for employees all across the nation. When OSHA contacted the company, Dad coordinated their visit. The installation of this sign over my father's office represented his aptitude for both understanding and implementing these new standards. He had a brilliant mind, with an IQ of 180, and, as a natural leader, he had influenced a vast, positive change for his company. Because the health and safety protocols were still in their infancy, Dad had participated in the pioneering phase of this initial establishment endeavor, and the wooden sign was a symbol of great accomplishment, direction, management, and intelligence.

A few years ago, I traveled back to that lumber mill, and lo and behold, the sign was still hanging on the front of the building next to that that old, abandoned electrician's office. The property was for sale, scheduled to be auctioned off in the coming weeks by a third party. I made a few calls about the sign, but I was met with the run-around, as the man who had previously owned the property could not grant me permission to take anything from a property that was tangled up in negotiation. He told me several times that he was "checking on it," but the words may as well have been, "I don't care about it." Each time I drove by that land, I looked out my window with a smile at Dad's achievement. His historical landmark. A piece of his mind left behind to remind the world what he had represented to those around him.

But one day, the sign was gone, and I wrestled with regret for not having been more persistent and firm in my requests to obtain it from the previous owner. I knew that, to anyone purchasing the property, this sign was useless garbage that would have been nothing more than an inconvenience to dispose of, and I was kicking myself for handling my request with such timidity. What I did *not* know, however, was that my oldest daughter, also named Althia after my late sister, was making calls of her own. She had contacted the new owner, snuck out to the property with a few assistants, and taken the sign down. It remained hidden at my mother's house for a while until a barbeque gathering with all the grandkids. When I was led out to the side porch with hands covering my eyes, I knew a surprise was in store for me, as it had been announced, but I didn't know the surprise would be that "THINK SAFETY" sign.

The tears I shed that day were for more than just an old piece of wood. I now had in my possession a piece of my father that remained, and the message to the world he had once stood for. I still have the sign today, and when construction on the ranch is complete, the sign will be given a place of importance.

While off the clock, however, Dad often lacked the same strict adherence to the cautious standards he kept at work. The night of the accident is the harshest of examples.

My relationship with my father was complicated, and that is another story for another book, but one thing I can say with certainty is that he knew the importance of safety. The accident was not my fault. Maybe I could have prevented the accident. Maybe it would have happened anyway. Maybe it was pre-ordained to happen. I will never know. But I was thirteen, and there was no way I could have completely comprehended the role my actions might have played that night in keeping Dad awake, and I have since then come to accept that.

Thinking back on those dark days now, this pill was by far the hardest in my life to swallow. This lesson is harder than any I've learned. Yet, the lesson of the Pink Pony is still present, both for myself as well as for any reader of this book who has had to face serious loss.

Sometimes the road of life is a joyous trip filled with laughter, songs, and happy memories of weird ponies that eat cigarettes and dog chow. It is during these moments that you find the pace of your trip especially comfortable, every road sign clearly visible and never misleading, and your "THINK SAFETY" sign hangs just outside the door of your office, directing you to protection and stability.

Other times, however, the road is thick with fog and your vision is impaired. You might be able to see the Pink Pony sign sparkling in the distance, promising your arrival to the next happy place, and then you wonder why, miles and miles later, you are in a dark forest on a back road in the middle of nowhere, your car running out of gas, your spirit running out of steam, and you're feeling scared, lonely, and unsure of where you could possibly be heading.

Experiences like these cannot, and *are not meant to be*, dismissed with a quick little Bible lesson you receive on a Sunday morning after a tragedy. It is easy for those who have not been through sudden loss such as this to hear the details and tie it all up with a Bible verse or some proverb that they expect will lessen the blow of reality. Those of us who have faced trials like these know that they are the hardest of lessons to learn and the hardest of lessons to even define. Quickly getting beyond the hurt and pain in those moments when the wound is all-consuming is not only impossible for the injured person, but the lesson is also obscured for a great time by confusion, doubt, numbness, shock, or anger. Summing up such devastation into some trite "moral of the story" does injustice to the injured person and, in cases such as this, it also delivers injustice to the lives that have been lost. Real, *true* tragedy demands the longest stretch of time for any lesson to be learned, and sometimes the lesson *just simply hurts.*

My memory of those days in the hospital is still surreal and mind-boggling. The word "loneliness" doesn't begin to describe how I felt as I lay in that recovery bed for what seemed like an eternity without being able to reach out and touch those I loved the most. At one point, my father's sister, Aunt Fern, paid me a visit. I remember very little of the visit, as I had not seen her since I was three years old. She resembled my dad's mother so much that when she asked me from my bedside if I knew who she was, I responded, "I *think* so." She told me she was my aunt, and said she would come back to check on me. To my memory, she never came back. It's possible that she did, in fact, return during a time that I was either sleeping or sedated to the point that I don't remember the visit, but other than this one short meeting with Aunt Fern, I have no memory of any other visitors in that first hospital in Needles.

I do know of one visit from my Aunt Juanita, though I was not awake or present when she sparked some controversy amongst the hospital staff. My mother was sedated and the hospital needed a signature of a living and conscious relative to sign the paperwork for the amputation of my broken leg. Aunt Juanita flatly refused to sign the paperwork, telling them that they would have to wait until "that little girl's mama" woke up and signed the paper herself. Needless to say, with both legs in full health today, I am grateful she made that difficult decision.

After the brief time that I saw my mother on the mercy flight to Maricopa County, they separated us again, placing my mother in her own room for further observation and evaluation. With both lungs collapsed at the time of the accident, it really is a wonder that she survived at all. It would once again be several days before I was reunited with her—and by that time, communication was limited as they had wired my broken jaw closed for healing. Finally, the hospital staff decided healing would be expedited if we were allowed to room together, so they put us in the same recovery room.

Although it was comforting to be in the presence of my mother again, and it's a kind of emotional relief I cherished, the setting was less than ideal. I can't describe what it is like to see your own mother's body and face in that condition, knowing also that her pain ran so much deeper than any collapsed lung, broken bone, or bruise could outwardly testify. We had *both* lost Althia, and my mother had the added memory of Althia begging to stay home before we left on our trip. Seeing her in the same room with me was just as heartbreaking as it was heartwarming.

After several weeks, Mom was released to go home, and the hospital chose to keep me longer in order to monitor my cracked hip. Another girl was placed in my room in the space where my mother had been. The girl had been involved in a horse-riding accident in which she suffered severe head trauma. Her arms were drawn up near her chest from what appeared to be muscle atrophy, and she lay in a coma, completely oblivious to her surroundings or her existence. I heard the staff using that word "vegetable" again, and that was when I realized what that could have meant for Althia. Observing the quality of life this sixteen-year-old girl was "living" helped me conclude that if *that* had been what they meant by Althia surviving as a "vegetable," it wasn't what I wanted for her. This was the only thing that could have been more painful than death for Althia. I couldn't wrap my brain around losing my sweet sister, but this girl in the bed next to me wasn't "living," either.

I pray that no thirteen-year-old girl will ever have to live such a horrible episode. Losing my father and sister in such a brutal and instant way changed my life completely. Everything about the mold I had become was wrecked along with the car that night. Emotionally, I was totaled more than the vehicle, and there was no repair shop for my brand of injury. I was ruined from the inside out. It was a wound, a *hurt*, that would persist for a lifetime, causing me to question every step I took and every decision I made going forward.

No quick-fix exists for pain like that.

And it never will.

If life were free of pain and heartache, the pleasant times could not be appreciated for what they are. So why do certain individuals face a greater degree of pain or loss than others? That question launches a million others, starting with the ever-popular, "Why do bad things happen to good people?" Ultimately, as long as we occupy this planet and until our souls ascend to the place of answers, we will never have a sound answer to questions like these.

And that, in itself, is a life lesson involving trust in something, or Someone, larger than ourselves.

But perhaps questions we *can* answer in this instance are: What happens to the mold when it feels wholly broken? What happens when we, like Job, feel destroyed to the point that the only words we find strength to voice are, "My spirit is broken, my days are extinguished, The grave is ready for me"? (Job 17:1).

When my leg set incorrectly at the Needles hospital, the medical staff of the Maricopa County hospital informed me that it was only after re-breaking the leg that it could be set once again for proper healing. Without that step in the process, I would have faced the rest of my life crippled. If I had continued with my leg in the wrong shape or mold, my body would not function as it had been designed. Sometimes it is only by our molds being completely reshaped that we, as individuals, can be "set" for the purposes God has in store for us to function. In no way do I wish to insinuate that God allowed that accident to happen in order to shape me for the future. However, only God is able to bring beauty from the ashes.

Things would never be the same brand of "okay" that they had been before. The car crash was irreversible, and the aftermath of lives lost was permanent. I knew very little about God at that time, and suddenly thoughts of spirits and souls and afterlife were flooding my thoughts with new questions to which I had never given much attention. My mom made sure us kids all understood that "there is a higher power that be," as she put it, so I knew God existed, but that was the extent of my knowing Him. And, as many of us know, it is frequently times like these when God meets you in your confusion and, even if only so slowly over the period of years, begins to bring you answers. Begins to glue your mold back together in a newer brand of "okay." A new shape. A new promise with greater strength, waiting to deliver new potential.

For the remainder of my days spent in Arizona, every time we passed the Pink Pony motel on the highway, I thought of those days just prior to the accident. I would have given anything to have the power to rewind and play out the circumstances differently, explore that building with my sister, knowing Mom, Dad, Terry, and John were all sharing a pitcher of ice tea in the desert heat outside our rented room. It was no longer a sign representing happiness and adventure that *will* be, but a sign of things that *were not* to be.

And it was not until a few days ago at the time of this writing that a blessing brought me back to the lesson of the Pink Pony. I may have been broken and nearly destroyed by that fateful night on the road, but God had not deserted me. In me, through and despite these circumstances, He was creating a work that would come to fruition in a way I never saw coming.

At the Apple Festival here in Missouri, I dressed several of my miniature horses in costumes and marched them in a parade with the assistance of my grandkids and many others. All of the horses were adorable, and all of them received a great amount of attention from their handlers as well as the onlookers receiving candy from the floats and parade participants. However, the horse of mine that garnered the most interest, laughter, and comments was Blondie, a gorgeous, twenty-eight-inch-tall palomino filly with a "dishy" (a horse term meaning "petite") Arabian face, soft brown eyes, and a flowing white mane and tail. A total beauty.

A few months ago, a couple of my granddaughters were helping out in the arena with some cleaning, brushing, and grooming. My older granddaughter asked for permission to cut the mane of Truffle, another mini I owned. I had made a deal with her that if she worked hard to cart-break this horse, I would give the horse to her, an endeavor she carried through without complaint or fail. I figured since the horse technically belonged to her, she had earned the right to style it how she saw fit, and a bad "manecut" wouldn't be the end of the world if it turned out to be a blunder. It would grow back. So, I granted her permission, and Truffle received a military/Trojan style buzz cut. Through some sort of misunderstood conversation, the same granddaughter took the scissors to Blondie, one of our main therapy animals for the Whispering Ponies

Ranch. Within minutes, the damage was done. Blondie's long, natural, flowing mane had been chopped to a four-inch, outrageous, perfectly straight line along her neck, and her bangs were squared like some modern punk/gothic getup, compliments of the resident granddaughter. Initially I was a bit shocked at the choppy new 'do, but upon hearing the other side of the story—my younger granddaughter also wanted *her* horse's hair cut—I understood how the girls had come to think I would allow this a second time, so I wasn't angry. Besides, I couldn't help but hear my words repeated in the back of my head: "It's only hair. It'll grow back." However, I had to be sure we all agreed this was a one-time thing.

Strict rules were thereafter set in place regarding the styling of Grandma's horses, and of course, the girls agreed.

People enjoying Blondie during her desensitizing training in the Apple Fest parade.

In the meantime, Blondie was scheduled to march in the Apple Festival parade, and it wasn't until the last minute that we came up with a plan for how to implement her new haircut into her costume. With temporary dye and horse paint, we colored her hair a bright, neon pink, and lined her lips with the most ridiculously adorable "lipstick" dye that curled into a girly little smile just at the corner of her mouth. From there, we put four or five pink hair curlers in her hair and paired her with the younger granddaughter, who walked along beside her in a pink house-coat with matching lipstick and hair curlers. The mid-morning-routine duo sparked the biggest reaction of the day. (At the time of this writing, pictures from this event can be viewed on the Whispering Ponies Ranch Facebook page.) People from everywhere flocked to her and adored her, and in return, she loved on all of them in ways humans cannot.

Her job and efficiency as a therapy animal was not tainted by my concept of what she should look like. If anything, she was more popular in her silly, unconventional way. I will always see pink when I look at her, and *for certain* there will be lots more shades of pink in her future.

I never saw it coming.

The Pink Pony of my past may never have transpired how I had dreamed it would, and that sign from the road always had a happy and haunting quality about it all at once. But I have a new Pink Pony now—a sign of a different magnitude to view in her stall with nothing but joy in passing. She's my horse of a different color. Capable not only of ministering to myself, but to people all around the world through our therapy program and Whispering Ponies Ranch.

When I look at the Pink Pony now with that choppy haircut, I know that time heals all wounds, and hair grows back. And just as Blondie's hair will grow back, my mold may have been distorted then, but I'm being reshaped into what I'm supposed to be now. Each day when I wake up and draw breath, I pray the shaping process continues. The woman I am today would never exist without fully trusting in the Man whose nail-scarred hands were shaping me even earlier than the night of the crash.

4

The Muddy Steed

*N*ita couldn't believe he had done it. It was the *one thing* he had been asked not to do. This underwhelming "cool cat" that everyone had been talking about was just as arrogant and typical as any other goofball teen, and he was not impressing her any.

For some reason, for some *crazy* reason, he thought he was above the rules, and now he had gone and ruined the outing she had anticipated for days, months, *years* prior to this event. Now, rather than to enjoy this day, here she was, jaunting off to find their parents to inform them that the cool cat had done something very uncool.

Furiously, frantically, she directed her horse across the dusty desert ground in pursuit of Clarence and Mom, not even attempting to disguise her agitation. Her horse obediently followed her cues, traveling around one building, and then another, then finally around the stumpy fence near the stalls. Her view of the open territory in the back of the riding range was limited by the cacti and harsh shrubbery known in many regions of Arizona. Still, her head whipped about in all directions, squinting in the blinding sun for any unusual movement.

"Clarence!?" she called at the top of her lungs. "Mom!?"

No sign of them.

Her eyes fell to the desert floor, hoping to catch a glimpse of fresh horse tracks. It proved immediately to be a silly thought. They were in a riding range where people came all day to ride, and recent horseshoe prints were all around her heading in all directions.

Turning her horse to the right, Nita picked up the pace a little. She had asked for a mount that was easy to control, and Nepravda, a white horse with black speckles, proved exactly that. As if he was reading her mind, when she slightly tapped his belly with her worn-out tennis shoes, he sped up only just above a trot, a speed she felt she could handle on an unfamiliar animal. As she moved around another bend in the terrain and past several other buildings, she continued to glance about frantically.

"Mom!? Clarence!?"

Still nobody heard her, and still she spotted no signs of horse or rider among the faraway tumbleweeds.

Why did he have to do it? Why on earth did this teenager have to conduct this preposterous display today of all days? Hadn't he been listening when the consequences of such actions had been announced at the beginning of the ride? *What was he thinking?*

To Nita, it didn't matter that he had a reputation of being one of the hip kids on the block. She wasn't awed by his popularity or reputation as the unpredictable and bold loner who had shocked and wowed the county. At this moment, all he represented to her was the showy braggart who proved his ability to do everything that wisdom and common sense cautioned against—and more importantly, he was the lunkhead who wrecked her big day!

Fuming again, Nita continued around the last bend in the range, and, to her relief, Mom and Clarence were a couple stone throws away, walking their horses and engaging in casual, get-to-know-you conversation.

"Mom! Clarence!"

At this final call, both turned their attention to Nita. Concerned, they trotted over to the stables.

"Wha's a matter?" Clarence asked.

Nita took a deep breath, calming her angered nerves before she spoke. "You won't believe it. He done did it," she began. "He drove that horse right into the thick of it! You gotta come help him!"

⚜

When my mother and I were cleared to return home from our eternal stays at the hospital, circumstances fell hard on Mom. Dealing with the loss of Althia was tremendously difficult for her, and I remember many nights she cried tears of unparalleled heartbreak that I hadn't yet observed from her, saying over and over again how much she wished she would have just allowed Althia to remain at Aunt Juanita's house. That, in and of itself, was sheer torture for her. But the life of a widow and now-single mother of three remaining children, all in their teens, especially in those days, brought significant worries. We had always lived on tight budgets even while Dad brought home the bacon. Now that he was gone, whether Mom was ready or not, the only choice she had was to find a way to provide for the children who looked to her for everything.

Today, if a woman remarries soon after losing her husband, many people weigh in by voicing their thoughts of a "proper" mourning period or question the woman's love and devotion for her late spouse.

But when I was a child, a quick remarriage was commonplace. Widows with children in society then had fewer ways to provide food for hungry mouths than the assistance available today, and remarrying—even soon after losing a spouse—was not only acceptable, it was often *encouraged*.

I know beyond the shadow of any doubt that my mother would never have allowed us to starve. She was a hard-working woman who only found pride in her ability to grant us kids the most comfortable lifestyle she could give us. However, times were hard, and when a single father entered our lives just after the accident, Mom knew how to recognize friendship, support, and camaraderie from him for the precious gift it was, apart from just a promise of financial partnering or business arrangement (which was also not uncommon for widows with children in that era).

For my part, however, I wanted nothing to do with Clarence…at first.

I came home one night to a scene I gravely misunderstood.

My brothers weren't home, and during that time, they almost never were, as they were older, and without Dad around, they had developed more active social lives. The accident had been hard on them as well, so nobody gave them any guff when they found activities to distract themselves.

From the entrance to our house, I walked directly ahead into our faded, mint green living room and found Mom leaning back on the couch, an ice compress on her forehead, moaning. Some enormous ox of a man I had never seen before was hovering over her, pressing the ice farther into her face.

"Come on, now, the ice'll help," he told her.

"Naw, now, get back, Clarence," Mom said, trying to push him away from her. "I don't want no ice on my face. It'll clear up by itself."

"No, trust me, the ice'll help," he said persistently, lurching his beefy hands back into the ice.

I had no idea what was going on, but from my angle, all I could make out was that there was a large stranger in our home doing something to Mom's face that she didn't like, and he didn't immediately stop when she told him to. She was pushing him away, and he wasn't backing off. The ice was an additional alarm for me, considering I only knew of its healing properties when used on an injury, and by the looks of this guy, he was most definitely strong enough to overpower and/or hurt my mother if he had been abusive toward her.

When he caught sight of me and locked eye contact, his gaze was intimidating to a small, thirteen-year-old girl with her leg in a cast. One of his eyes looked straight into mine, and his other stared off to the side of the room.

I didn't hesitate to intervene on the perceived confrontation. Mom had just been through hell on earth, and no big-armed, crazy-eyed outsider was going to be allowed to march into our home and call the shots. Without the slightest interest in learning the story behind the scene I had just observed, I started shouting.

"Get away from my mom! Back off, Mister! Don't touch my mom!"

"Nita, calm down," Mom said. "He's not hurtin' me. He's just tryin' ta help."

Seeing her jump to his defense confused me for the moment and caused me to delay my impending explosion. I watched as his burly arms pulled her into a more upright sitting position. When the ice no longer obscured my view of my mother's pretty face, I saw that there had been no injury.

Evidently, he *hadn't* hurt her, and had never intended to.

I didn't understand who he was or what he was doing in our house, but it mattered little. I had only been home from the hospital for two weeks, my leg was still in a cast, and something was wrong with Mom. I observed for a moment that whatever he was doing here, Mom was not in any danger, she was allowing it, and I had no say in the matter.

Still enraged by what I felt was an intrusion by a man whose presence was perceived as sketchy at best, I stomped to my room and fumed about for a few minutes, and then I heard the exchange of goodbyes.

As I learned later, Mom and Clarence had gone out on a date that night, and when they returned home, they had indulged in a few social mixers as they shared polite conversation. Nothing inappropriate ever happened between them. With everything Mom had been through, this had been the first time she had felt a semblance of normalcy, a familiarity to any kind of regular visitation setting since the accident that wasn't dominated by talk of tragedy. As they had continued to share stories and get to know each other a little better, the vodka and orange juice had been mixed a bit too strong in Mom's glass. Her head had begun throbbing, and Clarence, instead of leaving Mom behind to fend for herself to escape an awkward situation, found it his duty to care for her in the only way he knew how: ice on the face.

What appeared to me initially as a scene of bullying and calling shots has since become an endearing memory of the sweet, concerned, gentle giant who refused to abandon my mother in her discomfort. It didn't matter to him that she had a lot of emotionally hard nights ahead of her, or that she had three mouths to feed. Very early on in knowing her, Clarence loved her dearly, and wanted to provide for her and all her needs, including those of her children.

As was the way in those days for two single parents who showed remarkable compatibility, their relationship moved fast. But Clarence didn't think it appropriate to move faster than us kids would be comfortable with, so he made it the first order of business to start things over with me. When he asked Mom how that was possible, she mentioned my unwavering love of all things horses. There was a riding range not far from where we lived, and together they planned to take me riding.

Clarence told my mom that this was "a way to make it up to Nita" for how we initially met. When Mom shared this with me, I reconsidered my opinion of him. I saw this new man in my mother's life making *her* happy—making her think about things outside the realms of car accidents and death and doting over her like a prized jewel—it was clear he wasn't out to try to replace my father or order me around. Mom had no material treasures or inheritance to offer, so I concluded that this man must have really cared for my mom. And now, he was extending his time and efforts to befriend me by showing a genuine interest in the things I was passionate about. I figured a guy like that couldn't be all bad, so I allowed myself to start over with him as well. Besides, he had offered to take me horseback riding! That had gone a long way in winning me over.

Looking back as an adult, I can see that Clarence's conduct with both me and Mom were honorable and sincere. The circumstances of our lives after the crash were complicated, and he not only accepted that, but he welcomed it with warmth. His intentions were only to care for us, as well as my brothers, in any way he could. Following our meeting at the couch that night, I wouldn't have blamed a man for apologetically declining any follow-up date with my mother on account of her seemingly high-maintenance daughter. But not only did he come back around, he never required an apology for my blow-up during the whole misunderstanding. On the contrary, he saw *himself* as the one who needed to make amends, even though he had done nothing wrong. And how adorable that he would have done so by appealing to my zeal for horses, which showed that he wanted to bond with me as well through his support of my sincere childhood horsie infatuations.

I had ridden Coco, and that was truly a joy, but he was a small Shetland pony. I don't remember ever really riding a full-sized horse, but it had always been my dream to do so. For as long as I could remember, I had waited for an opportunity like this, and now the new man in Mom's life was going to make it happen.

I was told that Joe, Clarence's son, would be coming along with us on the ride. Mom had said it would be "kinda like a double date" with the four of us. This allowed Mom and Clarence to take their horses in a different direction and visit alone while Joe and I had each other for company. I went along with the date idea nonchalantly. It never crossed my mind that a double date between parents and their teens would be awkward, because that was not my focus. I didn't care if I had been set up with Santa Claus and his elves as long as I got a horse ride out of the deal.

The drive from home to the range was probably thirty minutes, but to me, it felt like a whole day's drive. On top of that, no one in our group had eaten lunch, so we stopped on the way for burgers—just another delay keeping me from mounting that blessed steed.

Eternity passed, and when we finally arrived, I stepped out of the car and took in my surroundings with rapture. Horses lined up just outside the stables and stalls, all saddled and ready to go. Because Coco had been the only hands-on experience I ever had with horses, I half expected them to be unpredictable and difficult to control. But each of these animals was clean, well fed, and poised, standing calmly and obediently near their handlers, displaying adherence to a level of training that promised my ride would be not only manageable, but perfect.

There were horses of every natural color, some tailored with a particular grooming style, and others left to flaunt their inherent flowing mane and tail. Such beautiful beasts. Any princess in any storybook from any library in the world would be lucky to even touch one of these gracious and dignified animals, and I was the lucky little girl whose entire afternoon was given to explore one small corner of the world with them to my heart's content.

I restrained myself from acting on the impulse to sprint toward the line-up and start asking questions. I wanted it so bad. My imagination had already erupted with scenes of my hair blowing in the wind, clouds of dust swirling up from each hoof as it struck the ground, and a triumphant fantasy theme playing in from out of nowhere as my trusted steed leapt over the cacti and brush of the desert flora. This was it! I was living the dream… If only Mom, Clarence, and Joe would just walk faster!

Once greeted by the handlers, we were asked what kind of horses we were each looking for. I considered this for a moment, and then decided that if I was to have the most ideal experience, I would need a horse that was easygoing and well suited for a novice rider. Then, once the horse and I got to know each other a little bit, I could increase the speed and fly away on a trustworthy companion or simply trot about appreciating the scenery, whatever flights of fancy struck me at that moment.

When Joe was asked the same question, his answer was cocky.

"Gimme the fastest one ya got," he said with a confident nod.

I was thirteen, Joe was fourteen, and even at such a young age, I had heard so many stories about this guy. I wasn't usually hard to impress, and I believed a lot of what I heard, but there was something about him that made me second guess the need to immediately jump on the bandwagon of admiration that fell through the surrounding area like a whisper of wonder any time his name was brought up. Still, simply asking for the fastest horse they had was not a crime, so I kept my reservation to myself.

When my horse was brought out, my eyes drank in every contour of its muscular shape.

"This here is Nepravda," the handler said. "He's the most easygoing and new-rider friendly guy we got."

I nodded politely, and then turned my attention back to my assigned horse.

"Nepravda," I spoke softly, gliding my hand along the curve of his regal jaw.

His name was like a song, inspiring fantasies of a golden-clad Indian prince riding toward the sunset of the east in search of anonymity and freedom from the pressures of the palace. His muscular physique demanded an entire volume of poetry describing the phenomenon he contributed to the world merely by existing. Like a Viking with tales of war. An animated suit of armor, stout and solid.

Reeling in appreciation and excitement for the adventure I was preparing to embark upon, I slowly stepped from his soft muzzle to his long neck, studying the line where his coat met the flow of his mane.

"You comin'?" Joe's voice rang out impatiently. Now it was *me* dragging on. As my eyes snapped away from Nepravda to Joe, I saw that he was already atop the saddle of his speedy mount. It was clear from his expression that he was champing at the bit—even more than his horse had been—to get to the trails.

I made my way to the saddle and wriggled my shoe into the stirrup. Having ridden Coco barebacked as well as saddled so many times in the past, pulling up into a seated position on Napravda's saddle was certainly a different feel, but doable. I waited for the signal from the handler that

I was free to go, and then gave one last glance in Mom's direction for her approval. She and Clarence were heading over to speak to us, so I told Joe to hang on for a moment. When they approached, Clarence spoke to both Joe and me, but his attention was more centered upon his son.

Very early picture of Tom "Joe" Horn and Nita.

"Now, here's the deal, kids," Clarence began with a look of warning. "You can ride all over the place out here a'far as I care, but whatever you do," he paused, made eye contact with Joe, and then repeated those words with emphasis, "*whatever you do...DO NOT* ride up over that hill." Clarence's hand gestured to a nearby mound of earth. I turned to look, making a note of its location, and then turned back to Clarence with full attention.

Joe beat me to the obvious question.

"Why not? It's jist a hill," he said callously.

"B'cause." Clarence's straight eye met Joe's with authority while his other focused on the stables. "There's a huge mud pit on th' other side of it. If you go near it, your horse an' you both are gonna sink in an' get stuck up to yer breather gills in mud. I don't care where else ya'll go ridin', but that there hill is off limits."

"Okay," I answered with sincere obedience.

"Sure thing," Joe said nonchalantly.

"I *mean* it Joe," Clarence directed one last time, his wayward eye narrowing.

"Yyyup," was Joe's response.

A minute later, we were released to the range. Mom and Clarence had made their way behind the stables, and I followed behind Joe, who pointed his horse in the direction of the forbidden hill.

For decades this story has been told and retold within family circles. Each time it is relived, it's equally hard to believe, and it always sounds like some contrived or exaggerated scene from a comedy, but I promise you readers, this is exactly how it happened.

Clarence and Mom went their own way after the warning of the mud pit had been given firmly and irrefutably.

I kid you not…The *first thing Joe did*, as straight as a bird can fly, was set off in a full gallop toward that hill! Assuming that he planned to eventually go around it, I followed along in the same direction. Watching from behind, I kept expecting him to hug the outskirts of the mud pit…but I was not so fortunate.

Joe didn't first assess the situation, consider his riding skills, and *then* attempt to show up his father's warnings by dabbling at the edge of danger… No, no, no. That would have been too sensible. Joe, with reckless abandon, straight out of the gate, ran his horse absolutely *head-first* into that mud pit, as if, with breakneck speed, he was determined to accomplish the most foolhardy, harebrained expression of absurdity he was capable of.

It was quite the performance…

"What in the world!?" I said, halting my horse at the mud's border. "What did you… Why did you… What in the *world*?"

I had absolutely no idea what this stunt was supposed to prove. And apparently, neither did he.

"Huh. Lookie there," Joe said, adjusting his wide-brimmed cowboy hat. He looked downward, gripping the reins, watching as the horse struggled for footing in the impossible, mucky depths. The pit was, just as Clarence had warned, an unquestionably futile setting for even the most agile of stallions.

I stared as both horse and rider continued to sink. Within seconds, Joe was submerged up to his knees. The poor gelding bore the brunt of Joe's decision, now standing up to the chest in sludge.

"What do we do now?" I asked, hoping for a helpful answer.

"Stupid horse," Joe deflected, shaking his head in frustration.

Knowing full well that it was not the horse's lack of intelligence that had led to this malady, I glanced about the area, considering my options. There didn't appear to be anything useful nearby that would assist in pulling a horse and rider out of a mud pit, so I continued to wait for an answer from Joe. He shook his head again as he slid from the horse, sinking in up to his high waist. The horse had stopped struggling and merely stood there. The whole scene was pitiful.

"Well," Joe said, "I guess you better go get my dad."

Slowly, Joe began to inch his way to the edge of the pit. Watching idly didn't hold any value at this point, and it was clear that with my leg in a cast I couldn't jump in after him or offer any strong arm for Joe to grip, so I made the decision quickly to go find Clarence.

It took a few minutes to find him and Mom. When I informed him that Joe had done ran his horse into the mud pit merely seconds after he had been instructed not to, Clarence's crazy eyes suddenly became a lot crazier. Of course, since he was on a date with my mother, he managed to restrain himself from a profane reaction, but excluding the curse words he likely would have released under different circumstances, he went immediately berserk with rage.

"I jis' knew it!" he shouted. "I jis' *knew* that kid was gonna run that horse inna the mud!"

Turning my horse around to follow Clarence and Mom back to the pit, I saw Mom looking both surprised and disappointed that her date had been interrupted so early, and in such a manner as this. For his part, Clarence was both aggravated and mortified.

Back around several buildings, through the stables, and around the hill we galloped, all the while, Clarence shouted about "that ignorant kid," lamenting that "you can't teach that kid nothin'" because "he ain't got a lick a sense"...

In reality, Clarence had always supported Joe like any loving parent would, and he was certainly not a verbally abusive man, but in all my life, I have yet to meet someone as sarcastic, exaggerative, and expressive as he always was. Sometimes during his most frustrated moments, it was hard to keep a straight face while he ranted and flung about his huge body in a fit of southern-drawl hysterics. The big teddy bear that he was, everyone knew when he got going that he was as harmless as a housefly and would never set out to hurt anyone physically or emotionally— including Joe—but when he had something to say, he never wasted time beating around the bush.

As the rhythmic gallop slowed near the foot of the hill, Clarence's angry bellowing grew in volume and intensity.

"Well now, Meathead! Are you happy with your little accomplishment!? Did this little presentation achieve what you hoped it would?"

Joe had nothing to say. Taking his last few steps out of the muck and onto the dry desert sand, he stood quietly and shrugged, probably knowing very well that no explanation or excuse would shine any brighter than his folly at that moment. As Clarence lowered himself from his horse and marched toward the pit, Joe quickly stepped aside to let him pass.

"Tarnation," Clarence went on. "Stupidest thing I ever seen. Just *had* to go showin' off. Just *had* to prove somethin'."

I glanced at Mom. She was as curious as I was. What on earth did this man think he was going to do? Why wasn't he coming up with a plan to remove the horse from the pit? Why wasn't he sending for help?

Trudging directly into and through the miry sludge, Clarence approached the horse, grumbling and hollering intermittently, waving his arms about in a fury. Then wrapping his arms around the horse's torso, he heaved toward the closest drop-off point of the pit.

I was impressed…and judging by her reaction and comments about his strength, so was Mom. I saw a sparkle in her eye as she observed his movements. He actually repositioned that horse a foot's length without the use of any vehicle or machine. *He was* the vehicle!

I studied the distance between the edge of the pit and Clarence with skepticism. Even if he proved able to pull that horse all the way to the rim of this gluey abyss, he couldn't possibly be planning to extract the horse with his bare hands…

But, as God is my witness, that is *exactly* what he did.

I remember watching his brute strength with awe. I had never seen a demonstration of such tenacity, such vigor, such brawn! With nothing but his bare hands, Clarence pulled that horse, literally hauling the animal five times his own size, to the shore of the mud. From there, he moved to the horse's side, wrapped his burly limbs under and around the front legs, and *lifted*! The horse's hooves caught the edge of solid ground, and after a brief struggle, the horse managed to pull himself out completely. Clarence followed shortly behind, covered head to toe in grime and sweat.

And then, as if we hadn't just witnessed an almost inhuman exhibition of strength, Clarence fell straight back into his casual parenting tactics.

"Joe, you've done a lot of stupid things, but *that* was a doozy. How dumb *are* you? What's wrong with you? You got somethin' wrong with yer head?"

Still Joe stood without a response. I could tell by his posture and facial expression that he was putting up airs. Despite how embarrassed anyone in his position would have felt, he played it off by his cavalier stance. I'll never forget how Joe looked that day, covered in filth, trying to act unaffected, like a sophisticated teenage stud while his father scolded him right on the spot in front of a *girl*.

"Naw, you ain't got nothin' ta say," Clarence waved his hand dismissively. "Just stand there like a dumb-dumb with your big ridiculous hat, thinkin' yer a cowboy. Go on, now! Let's woo the women, shall we? How 'bout we go find ourselves a cliff to jump off, too? Why don't we just get *real* impressive while we're at it?"

Clarence turned back to his own horse, walking him by the reins toward the stables. Over his shoulder, he continued to mutter.

"Typical kid. Always gotta act like ya know more'n I do about everything. I hope yer happy with that stunt you pulled. Criminy…"

It had been an event for sure, but thanks to Joe and his great descent, the entire joyride lasted five minutes before the rest of our time was spent rescuing horses and cleaning up for the afternoon.

Needless to say, Joe hadn't given off the best first impression. When he ruined my day and deprived me of my dreamy sunshine horseback adventure, I didn't care that he was the cat's meow to all the other girls my age. Clarence seemed like a nice man who held true promise of happiness and stability for my mother, but there would not be a second "double date."

Little did I know at the time, however, this "Joe" was still being molded as well, and he would become the finest man I would ever have the privilege of knowing.

For the next few years, I only saw Joe in passing, as he lived with his mother. Mom and Clarence married soon after the horseback riding day, and I quickly accepted Clarence into my life, not as a father figure, but as a big buddy who made my mom laugh. As time passed early on in their marriage, I found myself respecting him for what he brought to our lives, and our relationship was always pleasant, but he was only marginally an authority figure for me. I obeyed him as I would obey any elder, but I never saw him as "Dad." Nor did he try to fill those shoes. He was always "Clarence" to me. We were all happy with the arrangement, as it felt natural. Immediately after Mom and Clarence were married, the two of them moved, taking me and my brothers to Oregon. Joe stayed behind in Arizona.

I grew to be more independent. The safety blanket called "Althia" was gone, and I found myself developing into a young woman, left with no choice but to develop my own thoughts and ideas without her present support or approval. I had a few friends, but nobody that I felt close to outside of family. My oldest brother had taken to hitchhiking cross country for adventure, and the younger of my two brothers was always in and out of trouble. My family was dear to me, but I never hung out much in my brother's circles, and I had a hard time connecting to others around me.

I was awkward and misunderstood by the majority of the world most of the time. My hair was stringy-straight and "tow-head" blonde, my teeth were crooked because of a cleft palate I had been born with, and I was thin as a rail. Because of the accident, my mouth had been wired shut so my shattered jaw could heal, and for years following, the entire left side of my face was numb and slack. When I opened my mouth to speak or laugh, I looked like someone who had just been shot with Novocaine, and the effect took years to wear off. Without any feeling in that part of my face, eating was a whole new challenge, and I sometimes found to my horror that I had dribbled on my chin. My speech was slurred, and my confidence in making friends, talking to boys, or participating in group events with people my own age was now all but destroyed. In addition, the crash had turned me into an inverted emotional basket case, generating internal baggage, creating a whole other list of issues in regard to how I related to people from that day forward. The need for a true attachment to others was always present, but never fulfilled.

When Joe came down for a visit one weekend, he and I discovered that we had more in common than I had originally expected. He might have been the *cool* loner, but he was a loner just the same, and an authentic connection between him and his peers was just as difficult to come by as it had been for me. He was never left wanting for a girlfriend, as the line of interested girls seemingly went on forever. Still, though, nothing between him and the silly girls he had met had ever been genuine.

We were in so many ways polar opposites. The cool kid and the skinny nerd. But when the rubber met the road, we were both terribly lonely and living in a world of strangers. Getting to know Joe from this perspective introduced a bond that shaped both our futures. We were both oddly independent social anomalies where it counted, and because of that, we were perfect for each other.

My mom was married to his dad, and for that reason, Joe and I had always avoided having a romantic relationship with each other. But there were several significant factors that continued to pop up between us. First, he had never lived with us. Rather, he was states away. He had never occupied the same space as I had in any living conditions with any permanence, so nothing about our association had ever been brotherly or sisterly. He was just a kid who came around once in a while, and I was just that girl who lived at the house he rarely dropped by to visit. Second, there was absolutely no blood relation between us. Third, we were able to acknowledge that if my mom and his dad had not signed a marriage license, Joe and I likely would have hit it off based on our own chemistry anyway. Just because our parents had connected didn't mean we weren't allowed to. And fourth, we were both so painfully hungry for a legitimate bond, a compatible bond, with other human life, that when it arrived between Joe and I, we were both able to recognize a once-in-a-lifetime friendship and union opportunity for what it was. Once we talked it through, we concluded it was permissible to see where a relationship would go.

I didn't know his real name was Thomas (or as many of you know him today, Tom Horn) until the day we went in to the courthouse to pick up wedding papers. He had been nicknamed "Joe" after his grandfather on his dad's side.

And now, here we are, forty-plus years, three grown children, and seven grandkids later.

The lesson of the muddy horse is clearer to me now than ever. Don't judge a situation—_or a person_—based on early impressions.

If I had held on to the impression I received from Clarence that night he was pressing ice against my mother's face, I might have kept my mother from a happily ever after that she, of all people, was greatly entitled to. Had I held on to the impression I received from muddy Joe,

I may have always assumed he was just a silly kid without a lick of sense running around the neighborhood trying to impress people.

We often draw conclusions about the character of others based on something we observe. A mud pit. Joe's shape, his mold, as a young kid being scolded by his father and attempting to act casual was rougher than the shape I had concocted in my own imagination for the man I would someday marry. But, as was true for me as well, God was still working on Joe.

There was a board game that was immensely popular in my area circa 1967 or so, called "The Mystery Date," based loosely on the hit television game show *The Dating Game*. The purpose of the board game was to try to get matched with the ideal mate at the end. For the girls, there were five possible mates. One was dashing, wore a tux, and held flowers. Another was a grubbier looking fellow who was sweaty, wore overalls, and held various tools. The latter of these two was the less desirable mate to be matched with. But that is merely a reflection of the society I grew up in.

So many young girls imagine the tuxedo and flowers and charming smile as the ideal, when in reality, many times it is the young man who is most well-versed at sweeping the ladies off their feet who brings the most trouble. They envision a knight in shining armor and end up with a dud.

For *me*, I was given the boy who washed off his mud and revealed the shining armor underneath.

But in order to see these tiers of character hidden within, "Joe" had to have been given the time to show the next layer, and I had to be willing to grant a second chance.

And, for that matter, who was I to *him*? My first grand impression upon him was of a crooked-tooth slack-jaw with a leg in a cast. Skin and bones. A total wreck of a tweenage girl showing more concern about riding a horse than about his safety in a dangerous desert pit. Had he judged me based on who I was that day, had his eyes been scanning for the voluptuous prom queen with golden locks and a perfect smile, there is no telling where either of us would be now.

People think they know what they want.

People think they know what they need.

People think they know what other people can offer them.

But, people can, and do, base these "knows" on fantasies or preconceived ideas that are entirely unrealistic. We may want the man in a tux, not comprehending that the man in the mud is ten times the greater gain. We may fantasize about our hair blowing in the wind on our own Nepravda, unable to wrap our brains around why the event needed to leave its mark on our memory as a mucky ruination, all for the betterment of our futures.

Everywhere we go today, our modern society stresses upon our deepest psyche that we have to move quickly and make sharp decisions on a dime. Sometimes, the impact of these strategies upon relationships is catastrophically superficial. This is true now more than it was in my childhood. These days, all it takes is a misunderstood Facebook post for a person in our lives to potentially be written off for good. Relationships are not like fast food. We can't expect to place an order for a spouse or best friend and get what we want ten minutes later. What a calamitous state we live in as a fallen race when relationships are judged based on what we see immediately!

And this is an unfortunate truth both for romantic relationships as well as platonic.

The day of the muddy steed has taught me most proficiently that oftentimes we need to stop thinking we know what we *don't* yet know about people and situations.

Don't judge the man with the ice pack. Ice can feel and look uncomfortable initially, but it can bring healing like nothing else can. This person could end up being the element of stability you or someone close to you needs to have nearby. They could just end up being the brand of healing salve you can't find anywhere else.

Don't judge the man in the mud. Mud can be washed off, revealing surprising layers of character underneath. This person could become the best friend you will ever have. They could become one of the smartest and most profound minds on the planet, affecting millions in a beneficial and valuable ministry.

Your mold, your shape, is not perfect as long as it's still being worked on. Don't assume anyone else's will be perfect.

That imperfect shape you observe *could* just end up being the man who builds your own Whispering Ponies Ranch.

5

Shorty and the Little One

*T*here would be no ceremony. Nita would be married without even so much as rice thrown on her big day. Weddings usually required money as well as a circle of friends, and Nita had neither. Thomas Horn, who was until this point only known as "Joe Horn," was never attached to the idea of a big shindig anyway, so the courthouse vows would be sufficient.

In the meantime, however, there was the question of where these newlyweds would live.

Nita had wracked her brain for months trying to figure out what her options were for funding her first home away from Mom. Dollars had a way of disappearing when needs arose, and despite the money she and Tom had earned doing odd jobs, the day was approaching when they would need to iron out living arrangements for their new life together, and dollars were what they lacked to accomplish it.

Now, with all other options waning, Nita glanced out the window, sadness toying with the edge of her blossoming features.

Could she do it?

Sure, sacrifices were a part of life, but this one was *huge*. It would be for her marriage. For her future. For both of them. But still, could she bring herself to give up *this*? Certainly, surrendering this beloved chapter of joy in her life would pay the rent on a home and provide a little extra for groceries in those first weeks together with Tom, but Nita couldn't bring herself to accept that these precious delights were the only valuable trade for such an endeavor.

Maybe, though, she would find herself with no choice but to accept it…

✦

In the years following the riding day with Nepravda, Clarence made it his duty to keep an eye out for horse listings in local papers. Anytime he saw a horse priced within our means, he would drive me out to take a look. I remember searching a long time before we found anything. Those days are precious in my memory. Sometimes we would drive more than a hundred miles in one direction just to see a horse we knew was not manageable for our lifestyles. But each visit to someone's barn was an adventure, and I was never heartbroken when the deal didn't go down, because I knew Clarence derived as much joy as I did during the hunt. It was clear he wasn't giving up, so I had reason to feel each unsuccessful attempt was a potential promise for subsequent success.

Car rides with Clarence were met with exciting and sometimes comical outcome. No matter the time of day or condition of the road, he would hunch far over his wheel and focus on what was ahead as if every drive was laced with thick fog. He didn't just hold the wheel, he wrapped his left arm around it from the elbow to the fingertips, steering with far more power and intensity than was ever necessary to direct the vehicle. With his right hand, he was *always* cranking at that radio dial, back and forth, back and forth, fishing through stations for news or whatever interesting talk show he might happen upon.

I remember one particularly hilarious night. It was "bring your kid to work day," and Clarence had been cleaning at the school during the nighttime janitorial shift. The drama department was clearing out their unwanted props and costumes, and among some of the items the school was giving away were a few silly masks. One of these was of an old, haggard woman with stringy grey hair, heavily smudged makeup, and a cigarette hanging from her mouth. Clarence had given these masks to me just for fun, so when we were seated for the drive home, I had the masks with me.

At first, the trip was as casual as any other. The minutes flew by as radio stations buzzed in and out through static transition. Finally, Clarence landed on a broadcast that piqued his interest. Talk of aliens and unearthly, paranormal visitations flooded the cab of his car. He stopped fiddling with the control and leaned into the wheel. As the station's on-air personalities continued their discussion of UFOs and space invaders, Clarence was pulled into such a state of intrigue that he had forgotten I was there. Because he normally drove home after a janitorial shift without anyone else present, he slipped back into that mindset quite easily, concentrating on the broadcast.

I sat still and quiet for a while, but eventually I grew bored with the conversation happening over the speakers. Excited to find a use for my new costume pieces, I placed the haggard, bag-lady mask on my head and turned my attention to the scenery from the passenger window, not thinking for a moment that a silly mask would cause any commotion.

The corners of the drive were sharp, and at one point, I saw a pair of oncoming headlights. I now knew that the dangers of the road were real. The curve made me nervous, and I turned to make sure Clarence was focused on the road. The passing light caught my mask.

Clarence, whose brain had no doubt been plugged into tales of celestial beings, completely lost his mind in fear. His massive clenched hand lunged at me as he released a frightened yell. When he missed, he simply continued to scream at the top of his lungs and beat the back of the seat with his fist, in an attempt to absolutely *destroy* the unwanted passenger who had suddenly appeared from out of nowhere beside him. Whatever it was he thought was in that car with him wouldn't have stood a chance had it been within reaching distance of his bear-like grip.

"Clarence! It's me!" I shouted, pulling off my mask.

For a moment he studied my face. I saw his nerves immediately calming, and then, sheepishly, he shrugged and said, "Aw, well, I knew that… I knew it was you."

"You did not!" I said, bursting into a fit of laughter.

I cackled for the rest of the drive.

When we got home, I raced as fast as I could into the house to tell my mother all about it. It was hysterical, a big man like Clarence afraid of a withered little old woman in the seat of his car during a show about aliens. Laughter… Lots and *lots* of laughter!

For the rest of his life, he never lived that down.

Clarence was easily startled sometimes. Once, at the end of a haunted house carnival ride, a man in a werewolf costume popped out to scare him, and his reflexes took over. His fist again lurched out involuntarily and bonked the man on the head like a game of whack-a-mole, totally knocking the man down to the floor. During a later retelling of the event, Clarence said, "Well, if yer gonna get paid to pop out an' scare people, ya may as well be prepared to pay when you scare the wrong person." This, too, was a memory that always ignited great laughter in a group.

Clarence was always bringing something new to the table. Whenever he told me to get in his "rig" to go somewhere, I followed his lead. I was his little buddy now that his son was miles and miles from him.

One time, during one of our episodes, Clarence pulled over to the side of the road and gestured toward some watermelons that were growing in a field. Telling me to be perfectly quiet, he got out from his car, signaled me to follow, and jumped the irrigation ditch, sauntering silently like a burglar to the fruit. Piling as many as he could into his robust arms, I copied him curiously, and then we lugged our loot back to the car and raced from the field unseen. Clarence didn't seem like a thief to me, but I was going along with what he had told me to do, and there for a while I felt like we had really gotten away with quite the heist.

It became an excursion we participated in regularly. Clarence would say, "Okay, let's go steal us some melons," and we would come back with a haul. Later, however, after I had been worried about this illegal activity, Mom informed me that Clarence was friends with the owner of the watermelon field, who had long since given him permission to take them anytime.

Relieved that I hadn't stolen, and yet thrilled to have been a part of the adventure while it lasted, I had a good, hearty laugh. From that day on, Mom referred to Clarence and me as Bonnie and Clyde whenever we headed out together.

Getting to know Clarence was always a joy, but some of the greatest moments were those involving a trip to check on a potential horse or pony purchase. A horse named "Shorty" heralded from one of these escapades.

After the now-standard drive to view a horse advertised in the paper, when we arrived at the barn where Shorty had been stabled, the scene was less than impressive. Mud caked the lower half of the walls and several of the stall panels had fallen into disrepair. Shorty was listed for sale at a hundred dollars even. A hundred dollars wouldn't buy much in the equine world even back then, and he wasn't much of a horse when we first laid eyes on him. Skinny, full of worms, and covered in filth from his hooves to his thighs, this twelve-year-old, golden buckskin bay blend gelding with a black mane and tail measured a couple of inches above thirteen hands and probably weighed about eight hundred pounds. Standing at thirteen hands high or less places a horse in pony status, which accounts for how Shorty got his name.

He was barely a horse, both based on size as well as appearance. Quite pathetic, actually.

Nonetheless, we agreed to the price, brought him home, and cleaned him up. Shorty became my very first horse. (Coco had technically been a pony, and he had belonged to all of us. Shorty was *mine*.)

As a first order of business, Clarence taught me how to properly de-worm a horse, as well as how much and when to feed him. Shorty had come with a hackamore (a noseband, not connected to the bit), but as far as a saddle, bit, and bridle, I had to come up with those on my own.

Picking berries was a way to earn money in those days, and most berry farms would give the job to anyone willing to collect, regardless of his or her age. The picker was paid by the number of crates (also called "flats") he or she filled. Twelve hallocks (a small wooden basket that holds about a pint) equaled a crate. The work was designed in such a way that a picker could move at whatever pace felt comfortable. As for me, I picked the strawberries and blackberries as quickly as I could, knowing that even the fastest picker on the West Coast would still take weeks to raise the money I needed. The first time I had ten dollars in my pocket, I ran with Clarence to buy the bit.

Shorty wasn't ornery like Coco had been, but he wasn't entirely trained to respond to a bit, either. As if he was the master of his own destiny, finally freed from the muddy walls of his previous home, he frequently disregarded the hackamore bridle and decided to go whatever direction suited him while I was on his back, and he would not stop at the "whoa" command. As much as I loved just looking at him, feeding him, brushing him, and tending to his needs, he wasn't capable of becoming a riding horse without the proper equipment, and the berry-picking was my only means of obtaining it.

Berry after berry the flats were filled, and I eventually saved enough money for the head stall. After more tedious gathering, two weeks later, I earned enough to add the brow band and throat latch to the collection. Soon, I was able to buy the reins to complete the bridle. Each piece I had collected so far was a slightly different color. Somewhere along the way, I had also bought a bottle of black leather dye, so I could make all the pieces match. Months passed before I was able to afford the entire bridle, but lo and behold, when it was finally assembled, not only was I proud of what I had made, but Shorty learned rapidly to follow directions, becoming a very fine mount indeed.

By the time we were riding together daily, Shorty had filled out to his gorgeous potential. His coat shone with regular care, and although he was petite, he was slender, muscular, proportionate, and striking.

Around this time, Clarence had the opportunity to add another little horse to the property. This one was what they call a "few-spot," a term used to describe one primary color with freckles of another. This Welsh/Appaloosa mix was white all over with just a small number of brown and black spots here and there. He was also very small for a horse, but unlike Shorty, who was beautiful and grand, this newer horse was stout, had a squatty rear end, was strong as an ox, and was simply adorable. He resembled a miniature draft horse. Early on, I called him "Little One," and the name stuck.

Shorty and Little One. I loved both horses dearly.

For all the years I had spent wishing to be the girl with a horse waiting for me when I returned home, now, thanks to Clarence, I was the girl with *two*! As before with Coco, I nervously waited in anticipation all throughout the school day to return to my adventures, and they were many.

As one example, I had a school acquaintance named Judy. She was prissy, hard to get along with, and used to getting her own way. She had never really cared to speak to me or befriend me prior to knowing I had horses to ride, but the second this information came to her, she buttered up to me as if we had been twin sisters separated at birth.

I knew I was being used for my horses, and this irritated me. I was accustomed to being alone and unpopular, so I could take her disinterest in me with stride, but her faux niceties toward me I could not swallow. I was not about to be unwarrantedly rude to her, but if she wanted to play the fake friends game, I thought it might be fun to play along.

After her persistent pestering, I agreed to have Judy over for a horseback ride. Because Little One was somewhat fidgety and spirited and needed a rider more experienced with his quirks, I knew I was the only one who could control him between the two of us, so Judy mounted Shorty.

A train passing through our property daily at two o'clock in the afternoons spooked Shorty each time it passed. Knowing this, I led Judy to the tracks and wandered about, making small talk. When the train whistled in the distance, Shorty flew into his typical scare, racing away from the tracks at a full gallop. Judy yelled and pulled the reins, and as soon as he had reached the yard safely, Shorty came to a long-sliding stop—something I had previously trained him to do. Not expecting this method of halt, Judy flew off the saddle forward and completed a full somersault roll down Shorty's neck, with my "friend" landing square on her behind.

I knew I shouldn't have, but I cackled and guffawed until I nearly cried!

Looking back, this was a dangerous prank to pull, and Judy could have been seriously injured if she had flown off that horse the wrong way. However, at that time, all I wanted was for Judy to either like me for who I was or leave me alone. This little encounter ensured at least one of these two outcomes.

Shorty and I spent a lot of time together. Due to a lack of social activity in my life, as well as an ongoing disconnect between me and true friendship with other members of the human race outside family, I told Shorty all of my tweenage girl secrets, and he faithfully kept every one of them. I actually talked to that horse quite often. There was hardly a bad day, a broken-hearted moment, or a happy update that he didn't know about. He was, for all intents and purposes, my best friend. I loved Little One also, but there was an unparalleled camaraderie between Shorty and me. That horse brought me through some lonely moments, indeed. He was much more to me than a horse.

Shorty and Little One were not only my first horses, they represented friendships that Clarence had provided in my loneliness, which held a special importance for me. Althia was gone and would never be back in this life, but I was growing to function without her sisterhood, largely as a result of these four-legged companions. Their worth to me could not be measured.

It would be several years from the day of the mud pit to the next time Tom and I rode together. I was nearing sixteen, and Tom was almost eighteen. Little One was full of himself and could sometimes prove to be a bit stubborn, so, just as with Judy, when Tom came to visit, I was Little One's handler. I had already seen Tom's riding skills, and I didn't feel excited about observing another calamity, especially involving my own animals, so anytime Tom and I took to the trails, Tom sat atop Shorty.(Besides, Tom would have looked pretty silly on that squatty little Welsh pony with his legs nearly dragging to the ground.)

Our outings were somewhat uneventful, but never boring. Getting to know Tom had its own list of challenges.

He was confident and cutting edge; I was awkward.

He was well-spoken; I tripped over my own tongue.

He was surrounded by people who wanted to be his friends; I was almost always alone.

He was *gorgeous*… I was a skinny and plain.

There were a great many differences between us. Most people would not have paired us together in a million years. As we learned, however, the things we *did* have in common were by far the most important. Tom might have been trendy, handsome, eloquent, and admired, but he saw in me a certain complexity and seriousness grounded by the wisdom and maturity that life experience had forced upon me in my youth around the time of the accident. Having never established a connection to the world, I didn't value the same social nuances as the other girls Tom had known. I wasn't silly. I wasn't airheaded. I didn't demand any special treatment outside the realm of simple respect. I had no interest in flirting. I never felt tempted to impress anyone on the outside with false advertising of who I was on the inside.

I might have been rough around the edges, and losing my sister and father may have given me a few more emotional bags to carry than was flattering, but one thing was true: Tom had never met a girl like *me*.

The opposite was also true. I had never even imagined that the man in the mud would become my best friend. Looking deeper than most others had, I saw the most intelligent mind I had witnessed in any person our age. He had an awareness about the ways of humanity, a perception about people and circumstances that showed his ability to know when to invest his true self in someone, and when to let them view him from behind his wall of gallantry. He had a depth that promised security and caution instead of impulse, a wisdom to determine truth from deception. He was, more than I could have ever foreseen, a genuine soul, one who deserved a more profound look into his multifaceted substance.

A *companion*.

When he told me he wanted to marry me, I was floored! Tom could have had any girl in the world, and yet he had set his gaze upon me, a frail little slack-jawed weed.

We had no money, and putting on airs in a grand ceremony was not a priority. A wedding may have been what I had dreamed about in my childhood, but without Althia as a maid of honor on my big day, and without my father to give me away, our celebration was dead in the water. Tom cared nothing for a wedding.

However, there was the matter of where to live. I didn't dare ask my mother for anything. She was strapped as it was, and she had been through enough that she didn't need another burden. Besides, if I was going to be married, I had to start taking care of myself like any adult venturing from a parent's home for the first time. I was determined not to rely on Mom to carry me through life, and that was one thing Tom and I substantially agreed upon. Taking care of ourselves was a matter of integrity, and integrity was a significant step toward maturity.

Tom was working as hard as he could fulfilling odd jobs about the area. The meager funds he derived from such endeavors might have been enough to *maintain* a life together once started, but not to *begin* a life together. We needed at least enough to rent a place to live, and those funds weren't materializing. Finding a place we could afford that would allow us to keep the horses was, also, not practical.

Eventually, I concluded that I had no choice but to sell Shorty and Little One and use the money from the sale for my future with Tom. I hated it… I *really* hated it. But it was a choice I made for the beginning of a new day as a woman.

I remember the day I took both horses to the auction. Together, they sold for ninety dollars to the same family. It was difficult for me to do, but I was used to the process of letting go. And *this time* it was by choice, and for the greater good. I felt happy that they were going to the same home so they would still have each other for company, and ninety bucks was definitely enough to cover at least the first month's rent and then some, but I was still greatly saddened by saying goodbye to those four-legged friends.

After the bid was settled, I went to the stalls to say farewell. I remember sliding my hand along Shorty's neck one last time. I don't recall exactly what I said, but I did leave him with a few parting words and well wishes for his new home.

The lesson of Shorty and his sidekick Little One is one of sacrifice. I had so little to give, but what I had, I gave freely.

I gave something so important to me in trade for something so important to me.

Considering how youthful Tom and I were at the time, I was taking a huge risk. Like many girls transitioning into adulthood at the same time they take their marriage vows, a little voice inside me warned that perhaps we were moving too fast, and perhaps it would all end in disaster. My heart told me to plow ahead; my head reminded me that it may not work out, simply because although we were compatible for the moment, life had a way of throwing unexpected obstacles in your path. People's shapes and molds were capable of changing. Yet, at the end of the day, I realized that these risks would be there no matter what or who my groom was on the day vows were exchanged, so ultimately, my decision was to marry Tom. And I was not short-changed. My wedding ring might have been the opening ring from a tin can, but my future would hold unfathomable immaterial riches.

But, as I would learn, mine was not the only sacrifice to be made.

The ninety dollars I made from the auction that night went straight into Tom's hands. With it, he paid rent on our first house, bought a month's worth of groceries, and filled the gas tank. Shortly thereafter, he got a job working for a local farmer harvesting corn, green beans, and other vegetables. Once again, Tom was the man in the mud, but this time, the impression he made on his boss in that field was astounding. Gene Stockhoff loved Tom's work ethic from day one. All the grueling hours of manual labor paid off both immediately and remarkably. Gene saw a young couple struggling and extended his concern for us as both friend and mentor. In an unexpected and unprecedented act of faith, he offered to clear an acre of his land, install a septic tank and well, hook up the electricity from the road, pave the driveway—all paid for out of his own pocket—and allow us to live on his property without paying a day's rent. Tom and I gratefully accepted this offer, financed a mobile home (which Gene even co-signed as guarantor to the bank) with the money Tom was now making, and positioned it on Gene's lot.

We will never forget the investment into our future that Gene provided. And, as history will tell, we will never forget the investment he made into our eternal lives. He could have charged us to live on his land. He could have made *us* pay for the clearing of that section of his lot. He could have billed us for the septic installation. Instead, he sacrificed his own money and property.

Gene was a Christian—a God-fearing, sweet, and devout man who made it his responsibility to lend a hand to a pair of near strangers in need, and in the most vulnerable way. Had Tom and I the motive, we could have made life for Gene very hard. We could have seriously complicated his peaceful land with skirmishes or theft or parties, among a number of other things. However, Gene had seen Tom's layers. Gene did not need to give the man in the mud a second chance and keep an open mind. He had gone into his relationship with Tom from the beginning with nothing less than the best of expectations and the utmost of confidence. Tom may have been a teenager with a secular worldview, rough around the edges, but Gene refused to keep his eyes on Tom's uncertainties, and instead focused on his potential, on what his mold promised to be capable of in time.

In the novel *Les Misérables* by Victor Hugo, a man named Jean Valjean has spent nineteen years in prison in Digne, France, for stealing a loaf of bread for his starving sister. Marked as a criminal upon his release, he is turned away from all the innkeepers, and is left to wander the streets. Upon seeing this man in need, a bishop grants Valjean shelter. Valjean, in the middle of the night, steals the bishop's fine silverware and slips out of the house undetected, but he is then immediately caught by law enforcement while carrying the stolen goods. When Valjean claims that the bishop gave him the silverware, he is dismissed as a liar and brought back to the bishop to stand accused of his crime. When the bishop is granted a chance to speak, however, he surprises everyone—including Valjean—when he says that Valjean is telling the truth. He brings out two silver candlesticks and presents them to Valjean in front of the lawmen, telling Valjean that it must have slipped his mind to take the best he had given him on his late-night departure the previous evening. Valjean, the lawmen, and the others in the household stood bewildered, but the bishop knew what he was doing. He saw a potential within Valjean that nobody else was willing to see behind his spotty record and rough appearance. When the lawmen had left, the bishop rushed to Valjean's side, and explained the reasoning behind his generous gesture: "Jean Valjean, my brother, you no longer belong to evil, but to good. It is your soul that I buy from you; I withdraw it from black thoughts and the spirit of perdition, and I give it to God."

The book never explains where the bishop originally obtained his silverware and candlesticks. Had this been a true story, or even the slightly more elaborated work of incredible fiction, the reader might be inclined to wonder how important the silver had been to the bishop, who delivered it into the criminal's hands without a moment's hesitation. It could have been that he merely bought it from the marketplace during a regular stroll with extra jingle in his pocket. It could have been that the silver was left to him as an inheritance from a distant relative he had never met. It *could* have been that this bishop's mother, on her deathbed, rendered unto her then-delinquent son the most prized earthly assets she had ever owned during her poverty-stricken life, requesting that he think of God every time he used them at the table, painting an entire pay-it-forward back story of how this lad grew to be a bishop as a result of this gift and his mother's departing words. In the latter of these possibilities, there is no doubt in my mind that the bishop would have had to sacrifice greatly by passing along these forks, spoons, and candlesticks in the interest of leading a man to redemption and a life spent in service to God.

As many of us have heard this story, most are aware that Valjean is deeply convicted by the bishop's deed. He struggles for a time between his criminal past, a lost hope in humanity, and the one spark of light promising a new start for a new man, should he choose to accept it. And, as the book tells, he makes a profound change, becoming one of the most respected and God-fearing heroes in the history of world literature.

It all started because the bishop saw potential in a lost and wandering soul and sacrificed ownership of his silver as an investment in this man's life, and this man, this previous prisoner with no future, turned over a new leaf, spending the rest of his earthly days as an investor in those around him who were less fortunate.

Tom never stole from Gene as Valjean had from the bishop, but Gene did hand over to Tom his own archetypal silver, his own *land*, for the sake of investing in a lost and wandering soul and his new young bride. (Our hearts were greatly saddened by the passing of Gene during the editorial phase of this book. He will be missed.)

I sacrificed for what I believed in, and so did Gene. I relinquished ownership of my beloved horses—the horses Clarence had helped me obtain—never fully knowing how or whether the sacrifice would pay off in the ideal way. Gene sacrificed his property and personal funds, believing that these newlywed kids might make something of themselves if given the boost early on.

Neither of our sacrifices was in vain. Surprisingly, however, when God is in control, some sacrifices can bring riches that no banker or accountant or appraiser could ever assign a monetary value to.

Remember as you dance the waltz of life that people are watching you: what you do, what you say, how you handle yourself on the job, how you invest the blessings entrusted to you…how your mold evolves and grows through time. Remember that, far more importantly, *God* is watching you, and in a way no fellow human being ever will: He sees what thoughts are in your head, what you spend your time on when nobody else is watching, what motives you truly have behind what you do, the intention behind the words that come out of your mouth, and what is in your *heart* when you sacrifice something dear to you.

Remember that your investments in people, no matter the cost, will pay back tenfold over anything material.

When I sold my best friends, Shorty and Little One, in exchange for a future with a new best friend so many years ago, Tom did right by me to spend the money how he promised he would. And now, today, he has given back tenfold—*more* so in fact…by far. I have more than thirty miniature horses in my pastures now, each one of them just as precious as Shorty and Little One. Each one of them a friend. Each of them unique and beautiful, inside and out. Not only do they minister to me on a daily basis, but every time I attend a parade and see the smiles on the faces of people from toddlers to the elderly; every time I observe people connecting with an animal that gives them joy in a way a fellow human cannot; each time I watch a smile erupt on the face of someone for the first time in years as they reach out and touch the velvety nose of one of my little buddies, I am reminded of my own candlesticks.

My own Shorty and Little One, as precious as they were to me, when given freely in obedience toward an investment in Tom and ultimately in God, bought the rest of my happy life: a life supporting and participating in the ministries the Lord allowed us to be part of.

It has come full circle. Tom has honored that sacrifice and provided

for me every day and in every way since then, including establishing
Whispering Ponies Ranch. He may not have stolen silver, but, like
Valjean, one small investment, one small *sacrifice*, redirected the path of
his life from that moment forward, and as the phone calls, emails, and
letters pouring into our ministries today attest, it was a sacrifice that paid
off with riches that cannot be measured in this life.

6

The Bronze Clock

larence was a bargain-hunter, rarely one to pass up a good bargain if he could help it. He knew a thrifty deal when he saw one. Some might decide *not* to invest in a box of expired groceries in the closeout bin at the local small-town grocery store. Not Clarence. Those groceries were a great deal! Others may decide that an entire collection of every color of yarn you've ever seen is *not* worth a few bucks if you don't already need yarn in your life. Not Clarence. Everybody needs yarn! Many may *not* bid two dollars on a mysterious, taped-shut, brown box holding "miscellaneous goods" at an auction because they have no idea what's inside. Not Clarence. Two dollars for a *whole box* filled with surprises inside had to have *something* good in it, and if two dollars was the only obstacle standing between him and the glorious mystery of what the box contained, then it was a steal!

It was a beautiful day, Clarence had some time to spare, and just like the day he bought that entire case of discount Chia Pet pigs, his bargain-radar was buzzing as he pulled the car to the curb adjacent to the "yard sale" sign.

That was the day he found the clock. It was a bona fide, sixteen-inch, United Metal Goods standing clock with a brass overlay like those you could win at the fair in those days. Atop the base stood the face of the clock on the left surrounded by various riding gear and on the right was a saddled horse with a chain draped around his neck depicting fancy reins. The horse, riding gear, and clock face all stood atop a heavy plastic base designed to look like marble. Clarence was a man of good taste, and he knew immediately that there was a horse-lover in his life that would delight to have this piece in her living room.

It was, for both Clarence and Nita, worth it for him to drive all the way back to the house to borrow money from Mom. When the gift was presented to Nita, it meant the world. It wasn't just that the clock was beautiful. It *was*. But it was also the idea that Clarence had gone far out of his way to obtain it, adding to its shiny exterior a sentimental value that was incalculable.

Nita placed it on the shelf in her living room proudly. The way it caught the light was brilliant. It shone as if it were solid gold. The back of the clock had been cut and fiddled with to lengthen the reach of the cord, and that jimmy-rig modification made Nita nervous, so she didn't plug it in as it might be a fire hazard. As a result, the hands of the clock face remained stuck, frozen in time. That did not make the clock any less meaningful, however, and overall, it was a sweet addition to the ambiance of her home.

As she would later discover, this clock didn't need to tell the time of day. It was the only clock she would ever own that had a way of telling the time of life.

Settling into our new lives together in the mobile home on Gene Stockhoff's land was special in a lot of ways, and it represents a time I will always remember fondly. Before long, we had a little girl with the sweetest temperament. As I had promised my sister in my youth, my daughter was named Althia, but early on, we began calling her "Allie." I chose to stay at home with her and love on her every waking moment of the day, as well as provide meals and house upkeep for Tom.

Because Gene's field only paid during the harvesting months, Tom got a job working at a cookie factory to supplement household bills and groceries. As a result of an accident while Tom was cleaning a Hobart mixer, he lost more than half of his index and middle fingers on his left hand. (Perhaps the readers of this book who keep up with Tom's ministries, especially those that have been televised, have noticed his incomplete hand and have been curious as to how that came about.) But God was gracious, and our needs were met despite that injury. Before long, Tom was back to work full-swing.

I didn't feel the same sting of loneliness that many stay-at-home moms do. Sure, at times I still envied those who connected with people their own age and with similar interests, but since that was a social luxury I had never grasped, in comparison, I had more friends now than I ever had before: I had a little girl who made it clear with every hug that she loved me; I had a husband who was kind to both my daughter and me, and who was willing to do whatever he had to—even if it meant losing two fingers—to provide for us; and I had the beautiful brass horse clock that carried me with a happy thought throughout the day.

Allie's love for me was, like the horses I had owned, unbiased. She didn't care if Mommy had a grisly scar along her jawline, or that she was skinny, or that she was socially awkward, or that she wasn't a great cook…and *this* friend would grow on two legs instead of four and learn to communicate with me with words! From the very earliest days of her life, we bonded in a way I had never bonded with another living creature. We didn't have much in that first home for a long time except a few modest kids' books and a digital clock radio. By her first birthday, Allie knew every single animal sound and had already started to develop a vocabulary. By her second birthday, she had started role-playing with me just as I had with Althia as a child.

There was this game we played a lot during that time we called "Howdy Neighbor." Allie could barely hold a conversation, but at the same age her peers were making nonsensical sounds and toddling about, she would pack a bag for travel, exit the back door of the house, come to the front door, knock, and pretend to be my neighbor stopping by for a visit. The bags she packed were adorable, as they were usually a purse or suitcase bearing a small toy or a piece of clothing. Adults carry things like handbags, purses, suitcases, and briefcases, so she would too, if she were going to be an official "adult" for the game. Our driveway was long, and our house had many windows, so she was safe to go out the back door and make her way to the front under my complete supervision. Then, when her anticipated knock rang out, I would open the door wide, with mock surprise, and say, "Well, howdy, neighbor! It's good to see you! Won't you come in?" We usually played the game around meal time or an impromptu tea setting so that Allie's "visit" had a purpose beyond the front door. Once in a while, when our money allowed, I could spring for a package of Lorna Doone shortbread cookies to go along with the tea, and that made Allie's neighborly experience all the more prestigious and fancy. (To this day, Lorna Doone cookies bring back memories of those good old days.)

I had a whole life ahead of me I had to figure out for both myself and my daughter, and certainly at times that was a scary thought, but the connection I had with little Allie made up for our lack of social callers.

Once in a while, one friend named Faith, who lived just down the road from us, would swing by to check in on me. She never preached to me, never tried to convert me, and never even attempted to goad me into attending her church, but there was something about her countenance that I hadn't seen in many others—a "light," for lack of better words. Although we didn't spend a great amount of time together, it meant a lot to me to have the caring attention of a woman who had no intention of weighing my life's worth on my looks or ability to outwit anyone in a verbal challenge. Her smile was sincere and her manner toward me was gentle. That "something" she held in her regard to me was more than just intriguing, and in later years I would come to believe it was a certain anointing of kindness—the brand that comes through a genuine relationship with Christ. This friendship was perhaps one of the first pieces of the salvation puzzle put in place for me. Somewhere in the midst of this woman's candid concern for my welfare, the fact that I had been given some space away from the trauma of my past, the contributing solitude of my quiet home (and all the self-reflection that inspired), and the idea that I had to start thinking beyond myself for my child, I had come to question eternity with a new importance.

At one point, Tom brought home a used television set, which greatly enhanced entertainment for Allie and me. I quickly became used to whatever channels we had access to playing in the background as I cared for the needs at home. One day, when my daughter was about two years old, my attention was drawn in by a speaker named Billy Graham. I had seen him before, and by now the concept of eternal salvation was contemplated in my thoughts, but I had never completely given my heart to the Lord. I had felt the conviction coming for some time—eating away at my insides and badgering me to address questions of this mysterious potential afterlife—but because I could not see that Tom had any external interest in God, I had hesitated, pondering what it would mean to turn my life over to something larger than ourselves as a means of lifestyle. How would Tom react to this? Would he be threatened by my personal decision to invite Christ into my world and put Him at the forefront of my heart even above my husband? Would a day come when I would have to choose between Tom and God? Would I be sentenced to living a life of faith alongside an unbelieving spouse? What would all this mean for little Allie?

And what did all this "afterlife" stuff mean for Dad and my sister? Assuming any of this talk of eternity was true, what did that mean for them? Had they been welcomed into the arms of this "Christ" personality upon their death the night of the accident?

Quieting these thoughts from my mind as they occurred had not succeeded in keeping them at bay. The minute I went about my day, resolved to let it all work out on its own, a persistent nagging would materialize once again, forcing me to address these questions.

I know now that it was a gentle pressing of the Holy Spirit.

"You folks at home," Billy Graham had said, staring right through the camera lens into my living room, "can ask Jesus into your heart also. Committing your life to Christ is not limited to a building or an event. Just get on your knees, now, here, *today*, right where you are, and ask. Invite Him in. Do it now."

Not limited to a building or event.

That is what he said.

A relationship with Christ could happen in the privacy of my own humble living room.

That is what he said.

The brass clock remained silent. The deficit of the familiar "tick-tock, tick-tock" built upon the daunting silence like a hovering expectation. A lingering and pressing reminder that time, itself, was delicate and could deliver short of human expectations. A harkening absence informing me that, just like the crash of my childhood, "tomorrow" was never a guarantee.

The clock's hands may not have been pointing to the correct hour and minute of the day, but it had a way of communicating the urgency of that moment in my life, and its counsel was loud and clear…

It was time.

I still have the historic clock Clarence Horn bought for me.

It seemed simple enough, and the man on television was even willing to lead the people at home in something called the "sinner's prayer" that, according to this minister, would seal the deal. I sensed that a spiritual contract of such importance had to have been more than just mechanically agreeing to repeat words. I was sure the individuals willing to drop to their knees and say these words would have to put action behind their new commitment, and that was a bit intimidating. Nevertheless, I had set aside this internal prompting a few times already, and *if* there was something to this truth that Billy Graham was speaking of, *if* there was legitimacy behind the idea that God would "call" or "reach out" to people where they were—despite their imperfections(and I felt I had my share)—then I decided it was possible that Almighty God, the Creator of the universe, might, just *might*, have been behind the recent prod-dings my spirit had felt.

In obedience, I knelt on my knees in my living room, bowed my head, and followed in step with the prayer flowing out of my television speakers. Then and there, just like the preacher on TV had led us to do, I gave my heart to the Lord.

When I was finished, I didn't feel any different. I stood, shrugged, and contemplated the act.

Well, that's done. I guess God must be happy with me now.

What may have felt at the moment like a lackluster spiritual experi-ence soon turned into something far more incredible.

I remember once, standing in my kitchen cleaning up the dishes, the prompting came back again—but this time, it was not about salvation, but about plugging in to a local body of believers. As much as I may have embraced the idea of keeping my little dedication a secret, finding a church and attending even once without having talked to Tom about it could represent a level of drama I was not primed to know how to deal with if Tom should decide he didn't want his wife rolling with a religious crowd. On the other hand, I was nowhere near ready to tell Tom that I had given my heart to Christ.

Knowing I had few options, I prayed in faith. It wasn't a polished prayer by any means, but one from a new believer who had no choice but to believe that God would see past my clumsy verbiage and into my heart.

"God, I don't know what to do right now. I do believe in you, but I cannot force Tom to believe in you or accept that I do. There's no way around it. I need you to deal with Tom. Amen."

Those incredibly simple words in and of themselves held no power. The Entity I addressed them to did, however, as I would soon come to observe.

That very night, without a word from me, as casual as if it had been discussed a thousand times prior, Tom came home from a shift at the cookie factory and asked me if I ever thought about going to a local church. I picked my jaw up off of the floor and listened as he told me he had been thinking about getting plugged in to a church. Was the Holy Spirit pressing him as well? I believed so. It was the first time I remember seeing for myself how God could orchestrate communication among a married couple, especially one as opposite as we were. And of course, I was floored by the notion that Tom felt he needed a savior. Tom was independent and _so_ strong. Despite the fact that he was also humble enough not to flaunt his maturity and wisdom, his very nature as it fell upon others around him suggested that he had the answers to so many questions already and was confident in his own person to accomplish whatever was necessary in life. Why would a man like that presume to need intervention from something outside himself?

Perhaps it was because a wise man is also one who will recognize _when_ his own limited and human capabilities cannot provide outside himself, such as the concept of any life beyond this one.

In almost no time at all, Tom had embraced Christ in the same manner I had, but with a fervor that has grown every day for more than forty years. The small church we began attending became the foundation of our ministry years ahead. There was no program for its teens, because at that time, the only teenagers present were the pastor's children. Early on, Tom saw a need in that small community, and he knew that he and I were meant to fill it. Immediately, he enrolled in Bible school through a correspondence program and began his first ministerial studies toward the eventual goal of ordination. In the meantime, he and I served as the church youth pastors. Our group was small, but now that there were people in leadership, we expected more to be joining us.

For the first time in my life, ever, I had a place where I belonged, and Tom was a part of it. I knew God so little in those days, but if I had needed any proof that the Lord had been listening to me as I knelt on the living room floor that day and spoke my first words of faith, God had just provided it.

And then, as if I hadn't already been blessed enough, symptoms of pregnancy foreshowed another friend for me…and now a friend for Allie as well! While Tom was seeing to the final details of obtaining his minister's license, I was waddling around in blessed anticipation of what we hoped was a baby boy.

While out picking up groceries one day to feed Tom, Allie, and the unborn in my womb, I bumped into Faith, my friend from down the road whom I hadn't seen in a while. We greeted each other and shared pleasantries. Eventually, the question of what I was up to these days came up. With a smile on my face and joy in my heart, I told her that Tom and I had not only given our hearts to the Lord, but we were also in full-time, volunteer ministry. Her reaction blew me away. She was ecstatic. It was then when she admitted to me that back when she used to swing by my house and check in on me, she and her husband had made a commitment to join hands in their living room and "claim Tom and Nita's name for salvation and the purpose of the Kingdom."

Again, I was amazed at how this scenario was playing out. Not only had God prompted Tom to respond to an inner call, but this woman and her husband had also been prompted to lift us up in prayer for the Kingdom! Who was this woman, that she would care for me? And who was *I*, that I was worth caring about? I was a nothing! A nobody! Of everyone in the world that would have deserved the attention of Faith and her husband, I felt I would have been the least of these!

But, we know what the Bible says about "the least of these," don't we (Matthew 25:40)?

I do now…

My gratitude toward Faith and her spouse is truly eternal. The impression she left upon me has remained with me my whole life long, and not only have I never forgotten her, but I have tried to model my friendship after hers, hoping to touch someone's heavy laden heart with just a smile or a phone call when it is needed in the same way Faith, this remarkable woman of faith, had done for me.

As Allie reached her fourth birthday, her golden blonde hair and smile had a contagiously cheerful effect on those around her. My son, about six months old at the time, had bright red hair and a gentle spirit. He frequently found himself easily amused, rarely cried, and snuggled like a pro…until he got hungry. When hunger hit, there was no warning. His wailing was almost bipolar. It would come instantly in the middle of a happy cooing session and end just as abruptly when he acknowledged it was time for the next delivery of food. We had named him Joe, after my husband's nickname.

Sometime in 1979, a package came addressed to me. Mom had not called me to tell me she was sending it. Because it was prior to the widespread use of cell phones and answering machines, any notification she may have attempted to give would have been lost in absent ringing had

I not been home. Nonetheless, the package came, and I found myself digging into it before I knew to prepare myself.

At the top was a picture of Mom's parents. I took a moment to gaze at the people I hadn't had the chance to bond with as closely as I had wanted, and I felt touched that Mom would want me, of all people, to have this photo. It was a time capsule, an artifact of our history, and I was glad to have received it. I honored the people staring back at me and smiling, acknowledging that whether or not I had known them closely, I would esteem this lasting memorial of them for the rest of my life.

I smiled to myself and set the image aside, turning my attention back to the package. The next item inside sucked the air from my lungs. My heart started pounding, and I felt tears come to my eyes. With breath quickening, I seized the faded photo and held it in my hands shakily. There, in a dated picture, standing next to Mom, was Dad…

My *real* dad. The driver behind the wheel that dark night.

Of course I had thought of him now and then throughout time, as he had been an unforgettable person in so many ways. But since the night of the accident I hadn't actually seen his face. When I was informed of what he looked like when found at the site of the accident, I was so horrified that I unconsciously placed a cork in my processing capabilities and focused instead on those who remained. Dad's death had been so vicious and so instant that it took some difficulty to find someone who could identify his body. (He had a closed-casket funeral.) In those first few surreal days, the list of survivors had included my sister, so by the time my sister had passed away, my focus had been intensely upon her and Mom, and it never fixed back upon my father.

Following the crash, I made it my number-one priority to take care of, and "be there" for, my Mom. She was so heartbroken that I wanted to be there for her at all times. It seemed like only minutes after I felt she was taken care of in her new life with Clarence that I was getting married at an incredibly young age. Then, we moved into our first home and had kids almost immediately. Processing my sister's death had been the default of feeling the true ache of loneliness, the void of friendship she had once fulfilled. Not having her there to witness my firstborn whom I named after her, or having her shoulder to cry on, or her tears to wipe away as Mom and I were healing from our injuries had forced me to think about her night and day. Although I had never truly processed or grieved her death with any finality, I had faced her absence to the point at which I was able to tuck the dear memories of her into a happy place. But, as hard as it is to explain, I hadn't even begun to deeply grieve the father, the *daddy*, who was lost that night.

Now, here I was, years later, my pretty little girl singing on the swing set in the back yard, my baby boy on my hip, and my hard-working husband at the factory—and Dad had never been given the chance to see what I would become!

There was a strong cocktail of emotions. I felt instantly bitter by the notion that Dad had been taken from me before he would know me—*really* know me. My potential. My calling. The meaning of my existence. I had never been able to show him what his daughter was capable of. An entire lifetime altered by one poor decision to keep driving when safety could have easily been found after a few hours at a rest stop. I was angry, and not necessarily at my father, but because I had been stripped of my natural rights to have a fatherly figure in my life as a result of something that could have been effortlessly prevented. I was grieved by the loss in a way I hadn't been, even when the loss was fresh. I was a woman now. A mother. And I had never connected with my father beyond the age of thirteen. What memories *had* been made prior to his death had often been happy, but just as often they were fraught with anxiety, the complex details of which are meant to be told on another day, and in perhaps another book.

Seeing his face ignited a fresh awareness of all the memories we never made, and of all the moments of happiness we would never be allowed to create now that he was gone. My father would never bounce Allie on his knee on a picnic blanket outside. He would never play his fiddle for little Joe while he danced his first toddler boogie. "Grandpa" was not a title he would ever know or enjoy. He would not be there when Tom stood to be recognized at his ordination ceremony. He wouldn't witness me playing the drums in the worship band while living my pastor's-wife role at church. My life with Dad had been ended for years, and it was only just now hitting me—like a ton of bricks—the reality that I had somehow skirted until this moment. The acceptance of Dad's passing had been suspended and ceased to tick, just like a clock whose cord had been cut.

The brass clock made no sound in the background, which once again appeared to be perfectly appropriate. Father Time was prompting me again, defying his own calculated rules. The present time didn't matter…but there was no time like the *present*—to seize the *moment*.

Tears streamed down my face as I fought to control my emotions. And then, I did something that I would later on discover was just about the healthiest thing I could have done that day.

I took the picture in my hand and picked up little Joe, who was dressed in an infant's onesie with a replicated blue tuxedo print on the chest. He looked about the room curiously, sweetly oblivious to the tornado of emotions raging in my mind.

"Dad," I said, holding the picture to my son, "meet Joe. This is your grandson. He's a good little boy. Such a *sweet* little boy, and he almost never cries. You would have loved him."

I sobbed, looked over my shoulder at Althia on the swing set in the backyard and continued.

"I have a little girl, too, Dad. I named her after our Althia. She's the sweetest little girl. So cute. We play 'Howdy Neighbor' together."

Between my voice cracking and my chest heaving, I could barely form the words, but I forced myself to go on.

"I have a husband now, Dad. His name is Tom. You would be so proud of him! He's a good man. He treats me good. He works hard, he loves our kids, and he takes care of us! He's going into the ministry, too. We both are! I found God, and Tom and I have decided to help others with our lives together. You would be so proud, Dad. You would be so proud…"

On and on, through weeping and sniffling and blubbering and the wiping of tears, I talked to my Dad. I told him about my life, my children, my husband, my church, who I had become, who I was becoming…everything that had transpired since the accident. I finally had the chance to face—and reconcile—his loss through the introduction of my family and my life to his picture. And when I had said all I could think of to say, when the man in the picture had heard the summary of the world his little girl had become a part of, I let out a deep pocket of air from my lungs that felt as if it had been trapped for a decade.

"Well," I said, placing the picture back at the top of the box, "I'm gonna go now, Dad." My words—as well as my heart—had been drained. Closing the box and placing it in a safe place, I gathered myself together to face the rest of the day.

The brass clock stood motionless in the silence following, like a friend just as broken and dysfunctional as I had been. A *witness* of my most intimate sincerity.

I didn't know it at the time, but this one event brought great healing and acceptance into the troublesome relationship between me and my father that had been cut short years before. A huge weight lifted from my shoulders and continued to lift in the following days and weeks, an unseen burden dissipating more and more each minute. It had been time to say goodbye to Dad, and it was only through the supervision of another father, the Father in heaven who commanded Father Time, that I could have ever been ready to embrace the change within myself that trailed that incident.

I'm not really sure why I never hung that picture. Perhaps I feared another breakdown, or perhaps I felt what needed to be done was done. I can't exactly put my finger on it, but the photo was never placed on my wall.

Time again passed, and I had a third child, a little girl named Donna who was every bit as smiley and sweet as Allie, but with fiery red hair like Joe, but unlike Joe's hazel brown eyes, this little firecracker's eyes were bright blue.

I'm not sure which kid is responsible or when, but at some point in our simple lives, Allie, Joe, or Donna decided it would be a good idea to clamp a combination-dial lock around the hind leg of the brass horse mounted on the mock marble base. Nobody knew the combination, so that lock remained around that horse's leg from that day on. Although I knew the horse was only a piece of metal and, therefore, the lock was not something to get too worked up over, every time I passed the clock, I couldn't help but feel that he had a different look to him. What once was a regal and upright horse whose very stance whispered of confidence, an adventure waiting to begin, now appeared unhappy, like a horse in a fairy tale held hostage by the guards of his rider's rivaling kingdom. Never to prance again. A prisoner of war. Forever frozen in a scene of captivity and confinement just as arrested by malady as the silent hands of the accompanying clock face. As silly as it all sounds, the sparkling horse somehow held a little less luster in passing than he once did, and that was sad.

In January of 2011, some thirty-two years after that package from my mom with Dad's picture arrived for me, due to old wiring in the Missouri farmhouse Tom and I had just moved into, our home caught fire before we were even able to completely unpack. No one was hurt, but every single material item I had ever owned or cared about was destroyed. The house had been updated and remodeled beautifully before we purchased it. Supposedly, all the wiring had been updated as well, but we learned later that some of the original wiring had remained in the walls, and this is where the fire began. As the fire spread quickly, I remember scrambling for my purse and the company checkbook, and Tom grabbed his computer. Beyond that, it was clear by the flames pouring out of our windows that we would never re-enter that home, and everything within it was gone within the hour… including Shorty's bridle I had pieced together as a girl, as well as the photo of Dad. By the time the fire department arrived, their job was only to extinguish the flames from the wreckage. Saving our home was out of the question.

I have never seen anything like it. That house burned to the ground like a match, taking with it every sentimental memory I had stored up throughout my entire lifetime. Those flames crushed me that day.

The night of the fire, just like after the car crash, I almost couldn't cry because of shock. The next morning, however, tears flowed freely as I stepped around the outskirts of the smoking rubble, searching for anything that remained. Anything. I checked any box, any shelf, any broken cupboard that wasn't too dangerous to reach. I was determined to find at least one part of my life that hadn't been burned.

Finally, under a mound of charred containers of almost unrecognizable memories, I saw a box that had been buried under fallen bookshelves. The outside of the box showed less scorching than the others, so I pulled it out and removed the lid. There, inside, like a trapped pet waiting to be found amidst the debris, was my old friend.

The brass clock.

The mock marble base was shattered, but the clock was otherwise intact. The combination lock that had imprisoned the shiny horse for most of our lives was lying in the box, detached from the leg. The horse had been freed. It had taken living in a box for several years while we moved around, surviving the blow of falling shelves, and finally, walking through the fire, but the stallion emerged.

And when he did, he was unshackled.

For everything, there is a season (Ecclesiastes 3). There is a time to get on our knees and surrender to something bigger than ourselves. There is a time to say goodbye to those who left our lives before we were prepared. There is a time to thrive. A time to live. A time to cry. A time to grow. A time to rest. A time to love. A time to walk through the fire…

And there is a time to find our shackles on the ground behind us as we gallop to freedom.

When I gave my heart to the Lord, I had no idea where that one small decision, that small act of faith, would take me, what it would be like to surrender my mold to the then-unfamiliar Divine, or how it would impact my children. When I said goodbye to my dad, I couldn't fathom how much closure that would bring. In both of these events, a freedom descended upon my weary spirit and broke the chains that bound me to fear and uncertainty, delivering me to a newer, fresher, *stronger* person than I had been. But, just like the mightiest of swords, there was a time I had to withstand the heat, allow myself to be tempered in the flames of the Master Blacksmith's furnace, in order to emerge unshackled.

The brass clock is still with me in my home today. Recently we fit it to a new base, but the lock will never again be placed around the horse's foot. Instead, it will be hung nearby, in a place of honor and memory.

Why?

Because, there is—_also_—a time to place our shackles within view, to remember the captivity from which we have been delivered.

7

Sundance

*T*he medieval knights-and-armor theme of the restaurant was perfect for Nita's birthday. Lights were dimmed, romantic music was playing, real cloths were draped over each table, candlelight and flowers were gathered as a centerpiece upon every setting, and the sconces on the wall gave the atmosphere an extra fancy flare.

Nita hadn't remembered a time she had been pampered like this, least of all during an event centered upon her. She was happy not to have to cook dinner on her birthday, and it was nice for a change to get out, just the two of them, but this was more extravagant than she had expected.

Tom gave the details of his dinner reservation to the hostess, and nodded at Nita to follow. They made their way to the cozy seats in the corner and settled in, thanking the hostess as she gently laid their menus in front of them and informed them that their waiter would be with them promptly.

"My goodness," Nita said with a laugh. "You really went all out this time, didn't you?"

"Yay!" Tom said with a sweet smile. It was a typical happy-moment response he usually reserved for the kids upon their expression of excitement, but tonight, Tom held a childlike countenance, so his reaction to Nita's question seemed appropriate.

Nita didn't even ask whether they could afford such an evening. Tom had been "flipping houses"—a term he used for buying a home or commercial building in disrepair, having it fixed, and reselling it for a profit—something he had done in his spare time for a few years, and it was starting to pay off. Real estate values were up, the local economy was thriving, and for the first time maybe ever, Nita could just relax on a special occasion and not think about the bill. Tom was, in every way he had ever promised to be, a true provider.

When the waiter appeared for the drink order, Nita splurged and ordered a soda. Tom had his typical iced tea, and for several minutes following, they excitedly chattered over the menu, discussing with piqued interest all the variations of steak and chicken that were available. Forcing herself not to focus on prices, Nita chose a chicken dinner spread and then leaned back in her chair with a contented sigh.

Life was good.

But little did Nita know, Tom's inextinguishable smile held a secret that was about to make life even better.

⁓⊙⊱

When I was in the earlier half of my thirties, Tom took me out to one of the nicest restaurants I had ever been to. I can't completely remember the name of it. I want to say it was "McKnights," or something to that tone. He couldn't stop grinning from ear to ear throughout the entire meal, and even though I knew he probably had some gift for me that was inspiring his excitement, I had no clue to what degree his birthday sneakiness had gone.

Halfway through the meal, he presented me with a card. It read:

Roses are red,
Violets are blue,
I bought a new horsie friend for you!

Wait… What!? A *horse*? A *horse* was my birthday gift?

The dinner had been more than I could have hoped for, so when the card was unveiled, I had expected nice words, but this reveal was an outright shock!

The moment was overwhelming. I gasped, then laughed, and then, with a rush of emotion, I began to cry.

Since my kids had been born, I had almost given up on the idea that I would have the all-American barn-and-pony life. Such dreams were the things of children, and when I became a woman, I had felt it was my duty to put away childish things (1 Corinthians 13:11). That's not to say that I thought horses were childish for others whose lifestyles could support them, but that was not the hand I felt had been dealt to me considering our limited funds, three children, full-time ministry, and now Tom's house-flipping business. Owning a horse, in and of itself, was not childish. In someone else's life, the notion of a horse as a pet was perfectly fine, and in fact, I envied those who were lucky enough to have the spare time necessary to maintain one. But a horse in *my* life would be childish and irresponsible. The lesson of sacrifice learned from Shorty and Little One had taught me that horses had to play second fiddle to the life I had chosen with Tom, and as far as I was concerned, that life had bigger priorities, even though they had changed from needing money for our first month's rent to keeping my own family and home at the core of my focus.

I was a proficient housekeeper. I kept up the cleanliness within my home to a level that some would consider obsessive. (Looking back, *I* even consider myself obsessive.) The dishes were always done; every load of laundry was washed by color and fabric type, folded while still warm from the dryer, and neatly put away in perfectly organized drawers immediately afterward; the sheets and blankets were stripped from all the beds and washed regularly, and the window curtains were washed every few months; the linoleum floors sparkled; the carpets perpetually held vacuum lines, even behind and under furniture and inside broom closets(and I used a rug rake for additional aesthetic effect); not one knickknack on the shelves was permitted to hold a layer of dust; countertops were not only clean, they were sanitized; not only the toilets were cleaned, the floor and walls around them were scrubbed as well; and I saw to it that my children were always bathed, dressed in clean clothes, teeth brushed, hair combed, well fed, and in and out of bed at exactly the right times. I was so immersed in a world of housewife duties that I even polished the leaves of our plants with mayonnaise, a holistic and aesthetic secret that made the plants glisten from a distance while never harming the greenery. My house would have passed the "white glove" test any day of the week.

Often, I held these standards for my own pleasure, wanting to give my family the best of my efforts, set the ideal example for my kids, and give my hardworking husband a spotless atmosphere to return to after work hours. I figured Tom was working so hard and receiving such little pay that if I were to view my duties as a job, I had to be worth the potential salary motherhood and housekeeping would deliver, even if I never earned a penny for it. But these reasons were not the only motivating factor behind why I poured myself into my home the way I did. In those days, and especially in the organized church, a pastor's wife was not only required to be spiritual and raise flawless children made of gold, she was expected to fill a role as Suzie Homemaker, and the pressure was on.

In addition to maintaining my immaculate home, I was a full-time assistant for everything Tom was looking after, which was a list that only grew with time.

How, then, could a horse fit into all of this?

Yet, I had learned to respect Tom's lead. If *Tom* felt something was within our means, I trusted him. Additionally, he had learned that this horse fascination of mine was not something I would likely ever grow out of. So, between both of us, the investment in a horse was a glorious inevitability at some point, and it seemed as if my husband deemed this the appropriate time. Now, not only did I have Tom's blessing, but he had gone around me for my birthday and surprised me with the news that I was about to be a horse owner again.

When Tom told me how he had gone about finding and purchasing a horse for me without my knowledge, I wasn't surprised that Clarence had a hand in it.

After Clarence and Mom moved to Falls City, Oregon, the house they bought had been owned by the mayor's sister, and she had allowed her brother to board some horses on her land. When Mom bought the house, she and Clarence had agreed to allow the mayor to keep his horse there until he could sell it or find another place to board it. Of course, Clarence speedily informed Tom about the situation, and he took the opportunity to gift me with such a prize, making Clarence, again, the man with the horsie hook-up.

It was Bonnie and Clyde, back in the saddle again!

Clarence and Mom had invited one of their grandkids to spend a few seasons with them at their farmhouse. This grandkid, my niece, also loved horses, and had spent time with Sundance while it was still under the mayor's ownership. The idea that our family had already interacted with her was a selling point since we had familiarity with her temperament. She was healthy, physically fit, good with children, and had a workable disposition for someone like myself, who was just coming back to the equine world after a long sabbatical.

Allie was approaching her sixteenth birthday, Joe was twelve, and Donna was eight. All three of my children were old enough to enjoy the horse alongside me!

Once delivered, I witnessed personally that Sundance was everything the previous owners had promised she would be. By looks alone, she was only an average fourteen-hands-high bay horse with a black mane and tail, but her personality was gentle and cooperative. Those first weeks of owning her were thrilling. Barely had I read that cute little birthday card Tom had written for me that I was already closing my eyes and reliving fantasies of galloping over the hills, the sun on my face, arms stretched outward, my horse and I connected as one, flying through the wind and pastures. Age, as we had all come to find out, had no bearing on my abilities to snap back into the imaginative wanderings of the youngster within when such thoughts were stimulated. When all was silent, I could once again hear the promised clippity-clops of adventure calling to me from the horse that was now in my backyard. When I went to sleep, I could see Sundance in my thoughts, waiting faithfully for me at the fence. And when I heard her neigh from just outside the kitchen window, my heart leapt in anticipation of the moment I could next visit her, love on her, stroke her neck, and begin telling her all my secrets.

I felt like a little girl again...

When the first week passed and I had only saddled her up a few times to turn circles about the yard, it was no big deal. I knew there would be other opportunities. After all, it had been a busy week. The church had a lot going on and I had a sense of guilt about riding her on my own without giving the eager, pleading kids a turn with her. The kids couldn't have a legitimate ride until I had gone down the list of safety precautions and taught them the basics of riding, and that would demand my undivided attention.

When the second week was over and I had spent even less time with her than the first week, I knew it had just been a busy spell. I would find time to love on her. No doubt in my mind. Allie was athletic and well-coordinated. Joe sometimes had a mind of his own and could be unpredictable at times, but Sundance had worked with children and had already proven to be a safe companion to my niece, who was about Joe's age. Donna didn't know a thing about riding, but she was obedient, level-headed for her age, and respected safety. It seemed feasible that instructing the kids wouldn't be too big a feat when the time came. I just needed to remain patient...

When a month had gone by and we still had not ridden her outside the yard, I didn't lose hope. We *would* find time to spend with her. It was just a matter of time before things at the kids' school calmed down. The church's constant needs would soon dissipate some, and that would unlock some free time in my schedule for sure. Tom would soon be between house-flipping jobs, so my role in that would die down some also. Allie could help out with a lot, and Joe and Donna were old enough to self-govern their morning and evening routines most of the time. Although, dinner wouldn't cook itself. *That* was a thing... Laundry had a way of piling up quickly in a family of five, so there was *that*...

The bathrooms were due to be cleaned also, but, well, you know…that would only take a couple hours. So the following days looked good!

Yeehaw!

By the time I had owned her for six straight months and hadn't yet even ridden her out of the backyard, I was starting to become aware that poor Sundance was going a little stir crazy. Sure, we rode her now and again, and I thought about her *constantly*. I *so* wanted to spend time with that horse and get to know her, grow accustomed to her personality, and appreciate her the way she deserved to be appreciated, but again, life comes at you fast sometimes: Three kids… Full-time motherhood responsibility… Full-time ministry… Full-time assistance to Tom's real estate developing business… Running over there. Rushing over here. Dishes. Laundry. Allie needs a ride to a school event! Yard work! Phone calls! Joe's picking on Donna! *Errands! Car broke down! Donna's crying! Church carpet cleaning! Choir practice! Tom's home for dinner! BLAAAHH!*

Between all the demands of my day-to-day life, I had little time left over to truly connect with Sundance, and when I did somehow manage to squeeze in an hour when nobody else needed me for anything, she needed a bath, or her hooves trimmed, or the stickers plucked from her tail, or her mane brushed, and so on and so forth…standard large-animal maintenance. There was never—*never*—any time to develop a relationship with her, and had there been, I couldn't put my own friendship with her above my kids' interest in riding her.

I might have been a woman by this point, but some things never changed within me, and putting my own self and my own interests last was one of the items on my list that remained fully intact.

And *how could I* put myself first? How could I have saddled up my mare, asked Allie to watch her siblings, and go riding off into the wild yonder when I knew that the children I had left behind on my own selfish mini-adventure would bear sad faces upon my return? Would *they* ever get a turn with her beyond a few nervous loops around the yard? Would they ever be allowed to experience the same freedom I had with Coco?

Perhaps some would consider my maternal instinct overbearing, but I had good reason to believe that life was fragile, it could be changed in an instant, and no child of mine was going out of my sight on horseback until I had confidence that when Sundance sauntered back to the yard, the child would still be atop that saddle alive, and with all extremities in working order. I had never forgotten that young girl in a coma from a riding accident in the bed next to me just after the crash—the one the hospital staff referred to as a "vegetable." Too many things could go wrong between a horse I barely knew and three kids who barely knew how to ride. It just wasn't safe to enjoy her until we had learned to *safely* enjoy her. That was the bottom line.

So there we were. A horse forever at the ready, but the rider forever missing in action.

Around then, Tom began questioning whether he should continue pastoring or whether there was a better way for him to serve the Lord and reach more people. It's a story for a different book, but one of the best decisions he ever made was to stop pastoring and to start a Christian media company (including television ministry and publishing). To pay the bills, put food on the table, and finance the fledgling ministry during that time, we wound up moving several times in a few years. Often, we would occupy a home that Tom was preparing for resale. Living in one half of the house—with the opposite half covered in a cloud of drywall dust or glops of paint everywhere or holes in the walls—we found our- selves cramped. Each time we moved to a new place, we had to board Sundance at Mom's until we could resettle. In some ways, this was an ideal situation, because we never had to pay for boarding, and since my niece was still staying at Mom and Clarence's farm, she had plenty of free time in which to dote upon and interact with Sundance. At least while staying at Mom's, our horse had room to run and play, as well as a rider who would give her purpose and companionship.

However…there were downsides to the arrangement as well.

Sundance acted like any horse with two completely different handlers would act. Just about the time I had worked with her enough to feel confident placing my kiddos atop her saddle, she would stay for weeks on end with my niece, who would train her to ride with slightly more daring movement. That little girl was a good self-taught horse-trainer. I will give her that. The things she taught that horse to do looked like they came right out of a Spaghetti Western film. And if my children had also been experienced enough to participate in death-defying stunt rides, we wouldn't have had a problem. Unfortunately, though, that was not the case.

Sundance, upon her relocation to whatever new home we were settling into, had to adjust once again into foreign surroundings. She would have to be subjected back under my training, which essentially reversed everything she had spent weeks learning under my niece's tutelage. Old habits die hard, and it was a challenge encouraging her *not* to rear back at every utterance of "whoa," and when we had successfully reached a point when I was comfortable allowing my children to ride, it was once again time to move to the next house to be flipped, and Sundance would return to Mom's house—*once again* being schooled to ride daringly.

And my issue wasn't always with Sundance's riding style. Horses by nature involve a certain level of unpredictable risk when the *people* involved are not trained to handle unstable situations. I remember watching as my son was pulled into the middle of a kicking match one day between Sundance (whom he was riding) and a retired race horse that we had been temporarily allowing to stay on our field. It wasn't so much Sundance that had initiated the squabble, nor was Joe doing anything to encourage it. This other horse, for whatever reason, just did _not_ like Sundance. He was a mean animal to generally everyone, and anytime Sundance got anywhere near him, he launched into a big dominance battle. On this particular occasion, however, when this horse tucked his head and threw an angry kick toward Sundance, his hoof landed an inch away from my son's leg. Panic seized me, and I instantly intervened, ending Joe's ride and separating the horses for the rest of the day.

I knew then that you could teach a young boy to ride safely, but as far as teaching a young boy how to respond to all the potential risks while on horseback, it just wasn't practical with the limited amounts of time we had on any given occasion to prepare my kids for the sport. Raising a son without a leg wasn't worth it.

After a while, I started to have these warning feelings in my gut about the whole situation, even when that mean horse was out of the picture. A few times, Sundance had been allowed free range of our property for long enough that she had become "barn sour." When horses are allowed to roam for weeks or months without being ridden, they can sometimes stop obeying the commands of their handlers and run back to the barn of their own accord, even with a rider on their back, because they are used to being their own boss. They don't appreciate suddenly being under someone else's control. When this behavior sets in, it is accompanied by not only a lack of cooperation with the commands of the owner, but also with the direction of the reins, causing an inexperienced rider to pull harder and exhibit signs of stress. The horse can pick up on these stress signals, and that can increase the risk of injury. I had witnessed this behavior when Joe was on horseback once, and once was all it took. When Sundance started trying to buck Joe from her back, once again, his ride was over.

Overall, though Sundance was an incredible horse with a temperament suited to working with children, once she became barn sour, I was the only one in my family who knew how to correct it, a challenge to which I rarely had time to dedicate myself. At one point, when Donna was saddled up and ready to go, I got one of these warning feelings in my gut and couldn't ignore it. After the gut feeling prior to the accident in my childhood, I had come to respect it when something inside me flipped on the red light. At first I told myself everything would be fine as I watched Donna calmly trotting Sundance about, but eventually the warning overtook me to the point I ended Donna's ride as well.

As it turns out, my premonitions were probably God's way of warning me that something could go seriously wrong—not only if I allowed the kids to ride Sundance, but also if I let them even go near her once she turned south.

One of the saddest things I ever watched was the death of our little mutt hound puppy, Ducky. He had been innocently standing around Sundance during one of her prissy barn-sour fits. We were attempting to saddle her for a ride and she resisted, stomping about like a child, completely indifferent to what might be underfoot amidst her freedom protest. After she trampled on Ducky's neck, he let out one last yelp and was gone within minutes, and the first thing out of my mouth as I watched him die was, "That could have been Donna…" I must have uttered those words ten times or more that day. Joe and Donna kept begging me to call the police or the vet or someone who could help our puppy dog, but he was beyond help, and although I was shocked to lose our pet in that way, all I could think about was how relieved I was that if there had to be a tragic event in relation to Sundance's tirade, a child was not the hapless target of her careless stampede.

My relationship with Sundance was definitely not becoming what I had imagined it to be. Having responsibilities as a wife, mother, and business owner was a game-changer, and although I certainly cared about her a great deal, I felt that owning her was proving to be more of a part-time maintenance job than anything else, and the job wasn't paying. When it wasn't a time issue, it was a safety issue. When it wasn't time or safety, it was correction, and then retraining again. It simply never felt right from the beginning, and as much as I wanted it to work out, as much as I *fantasized* that it would, for some reason or another, I always had an inkling that Sundance was never meant to be in our lives. And yet, here she was.

This went on for around two years, and then we received the news about Clarence, an event that added an emotional encumbrance upon the ownership of Sundance.

Oh, how we wished Clarence had not gone down in that canyon alone!

Clarence and his brother, Billy, had gone deer hunting. Midway through their trip, Clarence spotted a deer at the bottom of a steep hill and told Billy he was going in after it. Billy was disabled, and therefore could not accompany Clarence further. According to Billy's memory of the incident, Clarence wandered for a bit in an attempt to close in on his prize, and then, abruptly, he lifted his hand to the sky as if reaching for something that wasn't there and fell to the ground.

Billy called 911, but by the time anyone was able to descend into the canyon and reach Clarence, he had already passed on.

I knew I had to be strong for not only the sake of Tom, who had just lost his father, and for Mom, who had lost a husband, but also for my children, who dearly loved the towering teddy bear they called "Grampa." No longer would Allie, Joe, or Donna be greeted at the door of Grandpa's house with "Here's your candy!" Tom would not be given another opportunity in this lifetime to "shop talk" theological theories with his dad. The hearty, boisterous, gut laughter that resounded through my mother's home was gone. The sarcasm and exaggeration that underlined every story he told would only live on in endearing memory.

The days of Bonnie and Clyde were dissolved.

The world would never see another Clarence. My heart was broken. His heart attack came without warning. We were *all* devastated. Once again in my life, there were no words… It had simply happened too fast and come too unexpectedly to process the loss.

The only consolation during that time was knowing that he hadn't suffered, and that his death had not been brutal, like my father's. Likewise, not a soul alive today would question where he is at this moment. Clarence is upstairs now, visiting with Althia and the saints, and I am ever grateful that we will once again be united. When that transpires, we will all three be in new bodies, capable of riding the bright, white stallions on the golden desert sands of heaven without fear of pain or death. I thank the Lord every day that Clarence was a part of my life, and even though I already knew that life was fragile, losing him so suddenly helped me realize another very important truth: The time given to celebrate the lives of those closest to you—fathers-in-law, husbands, mothers, children—is limited.

Following the untimely death of Clarence, my connection to Sundance took even more of a dip. The gift of Sundance had been the brainchild of Tom and Clarence, and I wasn't able to set aside the time necessary to appreciate her even before Clarence had passed away. Now, with

Clarence gone, I had less inclination to attempt a bond with the horse he had helped bring into my life if I couldn't do it right. Anything less than the proper attention toward her was an insult to Clarence's legacy, an insult to the Bonnie-and-Clyde bond, and I was underperforming. If anything, my personal care for her was already bordering on neglect in the area of true companionship. The idyllic horse-and-rider liaison was entirely nonexistent. It wasn't what Clarence would have wanted, and it certainly wasn't what I had dreamed about.

I recall one beautiful day outside the barn in the sunshine that hammered the final nail in the coffin for me. Sundance needed grooming, so I did the "responsible" thing, set the growing list of house chores aside, and set out to the field. While I was standing there bathing the dirt from my horse and bringing her tail and mane back to flowing status, Donna came out to play. She was running about here and there without a care in the world, as children do. I stopped dead in my tracks and observed her. She was wearing the same clothes she had put on the day before, and her long, red hair was so tangled it was almost matted.

I looked at Sundance, considered the profound reality that was dawning on me, and then glanced back at my daughter.

What—*in the world*—was I doing?!

Here I was, out in the field, beautifying an animal that wasn't even contributing to my family's quality of life, while my daughter was running around with dirty clothes and hair. This was *me*, Suzie Homemaker! The duster of shelves! The vacuumer of closet floors! The mayonnaiser of plants! The pastor's wife with the freshly bathed and dressed, well-presentable children! And then there was Donna, left to her own devices with a head full of tangles…

It was a whole new low for me.

I was taken aback by the levels at which it was so suddenly revealed to me that my priorities needed adjusting. I had to make a hard decision. I could either be a mediocre mother and horse-owner, or I would be an excellent mother who would wait a while longer to thrive in pony land. I would not, *could not*, allow myself to ride the fence between both priority lists. Life has limits, and time is one of them. Horses could wait, but my kiddos needed me.

As much as it pained me to admit it, I felt I couldn't keep Sundance. I felt I *shouldn't* keep her. She needed a home where someone had time to keep her in good riding condition, and in good health as well. With a heavy heart, I loaded her into a trailer, drove her to the auction house, and sold her to the highest bidder.

Saying goodbye to Sundance wasn't nearly as difficult as it had been with Coco, Shorty, or Little One. It was the end of an era, and for that I was saddened. But I wasn't losing a companion as much as I was giving a polite farewell to a duty. My ownership of Sundance had always been oddly detached. Strange. *Strained.* Not once in the whole time I owned her had I ever found the opportunity to even ride her out of the yard. There was nothing natural about it, and my priorities were more and more out of control the longer I tried to tighten my fingers around the desire of keeping her.

From Coco, I learned the lesson that timing is everything. Sometimes we are given a taste of the dream in order to keep the dream alive, but only with the proper timing are we meant to fulfill it. From the brass clock, I learned the lesson that there is a time for everything, including a time to let go and say goodbye when the stress of holding on is too great. And from Sundance, I learned that *when* the timing isn't right, and *when* you need to let go, choosing instead to milk the dream for everything its worth only results in a mangling of your priority list.

Discouragement is also a disastrous side effect of tightening the grip around an improperly timed dream-tease. Had I sold Sundance earlier, I might have only experienced a small slice of the headache pie I that I had been baking while she was in my care. As it played out, everything I thought owning a horse would be was tainted by the entire experience, and for years afterward. What was once a vision of grandeur became a ball of stress and responsibility. What started as a romantic idea ended in fallout. I had started to believe that *this* was what it would be like to own a horse, and that dread stayed with me until my kids were grown and moved out of my house.

Yet, I can't say I would have changed it. Had I not learned the lesson of trying too hard to make something happen even when the priorities were challenged, I might have tried too hard at a different time, with a different horse, and a different set of potentially dangerous circumstances... I shudder to think my family could have ever been hurt because of Mommy's horsie desires.

Priorities are a funny thing, really. When a time-consuming endeavor is not meant to be, it seems that all too often a schedule will never open up and allow for it to be utilized, unless the responsibility is forcibly carried out, in which case it is rarely enjoyed or appreciated for what it is. When a time-consuming endeavor *is* meant to be, somehow, mysteriously, things get done when they need to get done even when it appears impossible to accomplish all that is required. I now have two properties brimming with miniature horses today, and even though I spend almost every weekend playing with my grandkids and work every single day rushing around in an attempt to assist Tom in the several full-time ministries we have running at any given time, these animals are given my attention and training. Honestly, when looking at my to-do list on paper, anyone could see that there is just not enough time in a day to accomplish all of it, and yet, it gets done, and the miniature horses are loved and cared for. The very fact that this book is getting written proves that at the end of the day, from somewhere, time still lands on me to focus on the priorities that are important outside daily duties. Priorities in proper placement of our lives can be an indicator that the timing of everything is right. Priorities are the teacher, and we are the students. If we can pay attention in class and learn from the signs we are being taught, our future endeavors will be more efficiently applied.

Sundance was the last horse I owned in the earlier years. After selling her, I would not own another until we moved to Missouri around seven years ago at the time of this writing.

Our lives went on in the following decades without any tears from me regarding the inner little girl's wishes for a pony land. We were always a happy family, never dysfunctional, and Tom, through prayer and study of the Word, grew into a patriarch that the rest of us learned to trust and follow.

Our ministry continued over the years, and Tom went from being a youth pastor to senior pastor to author, which paved the way for his website, Raiders News Update, one of the first online Christian news sites to meet the World Wide Web. From there came Survivor Mall, a Christian preparedness products store we started from an empty bedroom in our home that eventually grew to a thirty-thousand-square-foot shipping warehouse (which was until recently the main funding source behind the Raiders News ministries). The launch of Defender Publishing, the book publishing company that has been the platform for almost all of Tom's writing as well as many other well-known names in the genre of biblical prophecy, was the next endeavor to spread the good news of the gospel of Christ. More recently, the development of SkyWatch TV became the focus of all our resources, the expansion of our gospel-sharing to network television, as well as other visual media outlets like ROKU, YouTube, and video streaming sites across the world.

Early in our ministries, during prayer time, I had a vision one night that Tom was standing in front of a sea of people—hundreds of thousands of people—telling the lost and hungry about Jesus Christ. The growth of his own God-inspired dreams and molding throughout the years would bring that vision into reality.

I was not the primary provider for my family. That much was clear. But as a wife and mother, I had an important role to fill.

When the apostle Paul wrote the pastoral Epistles, he understood very well the congregants to whom he was addressing his words. Perhaps he did not know that his sound advice would travel the boundaries of history and culture, making its way into the ears and hearts of mothers in the 1990s, but I fully believe that the good Lord ordained Paul's teachings to reach me when I needed them most. Some things aren't meant to change, and Paul's observations of proper lifestyle and parenting are timeless.

In 1 Timothy 5:8, Paul specifically drives home the lesson of Sundance: "But if any provide not for his own, and specially for those of his own house, he hath denied the faith, and is worse than an infidel."

How could I have continued placing Sundance at such a high priority when those of my own house were silently, in their own tangly-haired way, calling to me for immediate provision?

For some, this is one of the hardest lessons in life to grasp hold of. Our society garbles up and cheapens our concept of priorities on almost every television ad, movie, billboard, and poster. The "good life" is said to be one with perfect balance between our own needs and those of others. Sadly, there is no manual to tell us when we should be grasping on to our own dreams and when we should loosen the grip.

Another verse comes to mind that, based on the hearer, can translate into many meanings: "The blessing of the LORD, it maketh rich, and he addeth no sorrow with it" (Proverbs 10:22, KJV). Upon researching a little into the pulpit commentary of this verse, one of the most popular applications subscribed to by ministers throughout history translates: "The blessings in your life, when they come from the Lord, will enrich your life, and you will find no sorrow or discontent in it." This is not, of course, to insinuate that the righteous will never feel sorrow in the blessings of the Lord, because, as many of us have learned, some of the hardest challenges in life render the richest blessings through toil, despair, hard work, and faith in the midst of confusion. What I personally take this to mean is that when your heart beats toward a lifelong dream, it is *only* when it comes from the Lord and under determination of His will and timing that the blessing will arrive sweetly and without sorrow. In simpler words, it will *enhance* your life, not stifle it. Sundance might have been a great blessing to me in my life, and that gift meant the world! But out of step with the divine authority and His omniscient timing, she was stifling.

If a gift or blessing causes one to forget their priorities, it is not the blessing it appears to be. But one more lesson can be taken from my experiences of Sundance, and it is strong and invaluable: If I hadn't experienced Sundance, I wouldn't know a true blessing from a burden.

There would come a day when the equine world would *only* deliver blessing and happy thoughts into my life and the lives around me for the kingdom of God. And when that day came, it was sweetly and without sorrow. My life is now *enhanced* by my horsie friends, not stifled. Yet, only after Sundance did I recognize the benefits for what they were.

I knew not when I received her as a gift what kind of strain Sundance would place on me or what owning her would do to further strengthen the contours of my mold, but if I had it all to do over, I would live that era of my life exactly as I have—with all the little twists, turns, and mistakes exactly where they were. My priorities may not have been in proper order in those days, but I have learned to keep a sharp eye and evaluate them on a steady basis, and I owe that to the lesson of Sundance.

He who began a good work in me is faithful to complete it.

Sundance was a strain.

Sundance was a burden.

Sundance caused me to reevaluate my priorities…

Sundance was—*exactly*—what she was supposed to be.

8

Five Big Horses and One Big Injury

*F*or some, "a place to hang your skillet" was a clever slogan. A cute phrase. An endearing string of words to be casually slapped down in a sentence whenever someone wanted to feel they were executing maximum-level craftiness in referring to that warm, fuzzy, homey feeling.

For Nita, it was a literal goal.

Too many moves, too much transition, never any stability: That was the way of life, and she had tasted enough wavering for three lifetimes combined. Since childhood, the words "a place to hang my skillet"— genuine words of southern culture in reference to a *real* place to call home, words she had heard her mother repeat many times in her life-time of relocating—was nothing more than an elusive tease. Here, now, *today*, all of that was going to end. No more packing; no more U-Haul trucks; and no more "living out of boxes." So many times Nita hadn't seen the value of completely moving in to a home, dressing it the way she wanted or appreciating the sentimental items she had in storage containers, when she knew relocation was imminent. But this home seemed more promising than the rest. *This* home was going to be where she finally, after over forty years of jumping from place to place, would hang her skillet for good.

It was a modest lot with cheerful neighbors and was situated immediately next door to the Camp and Conference Ministries office owned by the church organization that Tom had pastored for many years. Within that same office was the state Women's Ministries department where Nita had been honored to serve as the young girls' ministries coordinator. Now, no longer pastoring behind a traditional pulpit, Tom was seeing to the daily updates of his Raiders News website and working in a leadership position over a major camping facility in the Salem, Oregon area. Both Tom and Nita believed they had heard very clearly that this was where the Lord wanted them to serve, and Tom's e-based ministries could be operated from anywhere. So, after such a long wait, Nita's skillet was calling to her for "a hangin' place."

Tom had known that it was a goal for Nita not only to settle in a home and never move again, but also to commemorate that commitment with a skillet-hanging ceremony. *That*, she said, would make it official. Once the cast iron was on the rack, no force in the universe, barring divine intervention, would have the power to change it.

She had made up her mind.

She had put her foot down.

She had stood the test of time and trial, and was now drawing a line.

She had said her piece and counted to three.

It was final. Done deal. *Never moving again.*

Tom, in support of Nita's adorable and oh-so-official observation of the settlement, bought and installed a sturdy skillet rack specifically fitted to that area of the cabinetry. In addition to the tried-and-true skillet that Nita used for most of her cooking, Tom had bought her a brand-new set of cast-iron cookware to be hung for the event.

With celebratory coffee brewing only feet away from her, Nita smiled and hummed a happy tune to herself, flowing about the morning as light as a feather. Allie, now twenty-four and married with a child of her own, and Donna, now sixteen, had joined her in the kitchen to witness the formality.

"It's just unreal," Nita said to her girls, a single, happy tear threatening to expose itself. "I can't believe it's finally happening. I have waited for this moment my whole life long, and it's…it's just…"

"I'm happy for you, Mom," Allie responded, retrieving Nita's "special occasion" coffee mugs from the cupboard.

"Me, too," Donna added, placing cream and sugar on the table. "If anyone deserves this, it's you."

Nita sighed happily and scooted the box containing the cookware to just under the hanging rack. "You know, it's just been a long road. I honestly never thought I would settle into a house with the intention of never leaving it. It was always just a faraway concept. I have watched as others have spent their entire lives in one place, making and maintaining the same friendships and being a part of one community with one vision for all their earthly days." She considered her words for a moment as she removed each piece from her new collection and set them next to the sink. "I know some people think that sounds like a silly goal, you know. Some might even think that living in only one place for a long time is boring, or it lacks adventure or something. I dunno. I don't care about traveling the world or seeing new places. I just want to unpack my life for a change."

"I get it," Allie laughed. "Don't forget, that has been *my* life as well."

They shared a chuckle as Nita set the empty box around the corner out of the way and approached the rack contemplatively. "I know it makes the most sense to place the larger skillets in the back and the smallest in the front, but I think I'm gonna do the opposite, because then the ones I use the most often will be the easiest to reach. What do you guys think?"

"It's your house, Mom," Allie said. "Arrange it however you want."

"It would look more 'Home and Gardens' the other way, though." Nita looked at Donna for her input.

"Nah," came Donna's usual sarcastic and carefree response. "It's not like people are going to judge you by your skillet rack, and if they do, well…meh."

The coffee pot gurgled its last drops. Donna reached for the pot and filled the mugs, and then smiled at Nita with a nod.

"Well, here we go, then," Nita said, lifting the smallest skillet and hanging it on the farthest row back. "There's one!"

"That's so happy!" Allie giggled and clapped with childlike excitement.

Nita took a tiny sip from her steaming mug and then resumed. "Let's see… I think this one will go next."

Hanging the next skillet, she glanced down at her coffee and shook her head. Suddenly, the drink in her hand didn't matter. Now that the moment was here, she couldn't bring herself to slow down the process. Like a child on Christmas morning, surrounded by the rapturous eye-candy of sparkling red and green presents, the rack was enticing her to rip into the symbolic gift of permanence…and far be it for her to delay this experience any longer. Forty-plus years had been long enough. When all the pans were hung how she wanted them, *then* she would sit down at the table with her daughters and enjoy the view.

Setting her mug out of the way, she grabbed one skillet after another, hanging and rehanging them: This one first. Then that one. This one back there. Bring this one up front. Nope, that one would rarely be used, so it should go back to the back...

When all the skillets that she had collected, from old to new, were hung in place, Nita wrapped her fingers around the handle of her favorite and most trusted cooking piece. It was the largest, heaviest, and most frequently used kitchen utensil she owned.

This was it. The last in the lineup. The old reliable. The skillet that had been waiting with Nita for decades to hang in a place of honor. She had fried many a tater in that skillet, and the "hangin' day" had arrived.

"Here we go, guys," Nita said, lifting the handle to its hook. Slowly, respectfully, Nita released the pan and watched as it swayed just slightly. About half a minute later, when the skillet hung still, she turned to her daughters who were beaming with reassuring enthusiasm.

"Ta-da!" Nita took a deep, meaningful breath. One arm stretched outward to the rack proudly, presenting the end of the ceremony, and the beginning of a new life.

It was done. The skillet was hung. The tape was cut. The rite of passage to stability was paid for and the receipt was framed.

Nita's days of waiting were over. Like a deer panting for the waters, she drank in the moment, allowing her heart to experience the renewal of hope.

For a moment, Allie and Donna sat quietly, allowing their mother to savor the taste of sweet beginnings.

But then, Allie gasped...

"Mom, *MOVE OUTTA THE WAY!*" Donna shouted, jumping from her seat at the table and spilling her coffee.

Nita spun on her heel and jumped backward. The skillets had been unevenly distributed, the heaviest pans at the front, causing the whole rack to flip from its mounting.

As if in slow motion, Nita watched as every single piece from her cookware collection plummeted one by one from largest to smallest, cast iron upon cast iron upon hard kitchen flooring, clanging about the otherwise peaceful atmosphere like an uninhibited, raging bull in a fragile china shop. It was the loudest and most abrasive crashing noise she had ever witnessed and the calamitous explosion of sound seemed to go on for hours.

Nita lifted her hands to her ears, but the gesture mattered little, as the noise was ear-splittingly penetrating. With every clash, a small chunk of the hopefulness she held seconds prior was shattered, until the last and final skillet spun to a stop face-down in front of the others.

Silence followed.

Nobody moved.

Coffee dripped from the table's edge.

Allie and Donna's eyes fixed on Nita, while Nita's were turned downward in disbelief.

And then, her vision was blurred by the onset of tears.

When it seemed appropriate, Donna intervened.

"It doesn't mean anything, Mom," Donna said, springing to the sink for a rag. Quickly, she returned to the table and started mopping up the spill. "Listen to me. It doesn't mean anything. It's just a coincidence. The top of the rack needs to be weighted down, that's all. Dad will be able to fix it."

"Yeah, but...I... I don't know what to say. I just...don't know what to say."

Allie lowered herself to the floor near the cabinets and started lifting the pans to the sink for washing.

"Why would this happen?" Nita asked. "After all this time, I—"

"No, no, no," Donna scolded. "Don't do that. Don't do the thing. This isn't a 'sign,' Mom. It doesn't mean anything. Listen to me, Mom. This ain't nothin'. Dad's gonna fix it."

***

But it *was* a sign. And it wasn't just that the skillets fell. The other skillets in my collection wouldn't have fallen by themselves. Had I organized them in any other way, they would have remained. Had I only hung my favorite, it, too, would have remained, but I had to hang them all. It wasn't until I had hoisted that monster skillet onto its hook—the skillet I had been waiting for *years* to hang—that the distribution of weight was too much for the rack to hold. When they did come crashing down, the noise was so loud that the rest of the house vibrated. It was alarming and assaulting to my nerves. So much weight piling up on the floor all at once.

I knew that the rack could be easily fixed. It was just a matter of fixing a counterweight, arranging the pans differently, or even drilling the back of the rack into the rear wall (which is what Tom did in the following days). Within the week, the skillets were all rehung. But I had received, loud and clear, what I believe to have been God's personal message to me:

"I am in control, and you'll hang you skillets when *I* say you'll hang your skillets. I am still working on you. Reconsider your concept of settling. Is this place *really* what you want? What about the place I have in store for you? I know the desires of your heart. Be patient. The fruit you pick from my tree will taste the sweetest only when it is ripened."

It was true that Tom and I had, in fact, been called to that location to serve on the Camp and Conference Ministries (CCM) board. It was also true that I was meant to be stationed in the Oregon State Headquarters of the church organization Tom had been a preacher of. But that did *not* mean that I was meant to settle there for the rest of my life.

We had lived there only a couple of months when Tom was approached by CCM with a proposition. The youth camp they owned near Three Sisters Mountain in central Oregon had fallen into great disrepair, and the turnover rate of management was at an all-time high as a result of an overwhelming workload. Because of the condition of the campgrounds, the camp administrators found themselves on their days off resolving leaky roofs; the foodservice staff were spending more and more time trying to fix the tiny, broken refrigerators they were operating out of than feeding the hundreds of campers at any given meal; the custodial staff were too busy repairing toilets to properly clean them; and the maintenance man had to depend on untrained staff at the facility to assist him in tinkering the plumbing, machinery, and electric because the list of needs were more than he, alone, could see to.

Tom had a lot of experience in construction and remodeling, so the CCM board asked Tom and me to pack and head up the mountain for the duration of a one-year volunteer commitment to improve the grounds and bring everything back to working order. We had reservations at first, but eventually Tom felt convicted about assisting where his skillset was needed the most, and we headed up to the youth camp in obedience. We planned to complete this one-year term and return to our home near Salem.

Our one-year commitment became nearly seven years, because Tom and I both felt that simply returning the place to functioning capabilities came up short of its potential. The place was beautiful, and we saw many souls healed during our time there. We felt that the promise of rehabilitation for so many who visited that camp deserved to give those grounds the best we could give it, so after we had patched the bare essentials, we began a long (and sometimes grueling) process toward optimal operation. In the beginning, there was skeletal staff because there was skeletal funding. Tom *aggressively* sought to acquire more incoming camp groups, and slowly the cash flow allowed for additional remodeling and building. Over time, additional staff were hired on and trained, propelling the building projects by leaps and bounds. Among them were Allie with her family, Joe with his wife, and Donna, who was still single at the time.

Our family could have *never* done it alone, but thanks to the Lord and the wonderful people He brought to the camp, by the time we left, the facility was fully repaired and operational with major new buildings erected to accommodate diverse retreat groups. The conference grounds had achieved American Camping Association accreditation (the highest standard of safety procedures and operational policies a campground can attain), and Tom was able to raise hundreds of thousands of dollars in cash from charitable trusts and millions of dollars of in-kind donations. Camp Davidson arose to become the premier retreat of its kind in Oregon with a backlog of user groups wanting to book dates.

Yet as successful as it was, from the minute we arrived at the camp until the moment we left, I always knew it was no place to hang my skillet. For certain, the place was a temporary stop on the journey to settling down.

As soon as we felt we had accomplished all we had gone there to do, we gave our notice and awaited Tom's replacement as executive director. By then, however, we were eager to return to Tom's personal ministries. Although we had moved to Salem initially, it was clear the real need was for the retreat facility in central Oregon, so we never returned to our home in Salem except to sell it. The CCM board gave us a farewell with their blessings, and we moved to a small city near Gresham, Oregon.

It was, once again, a temporary stop on the journey to the skillet house.

During this time Tom focused primarily on operating his Christian news service and publishing house, and on launching Survivor Mall. In those days, Survivor Mall was run out of our home, and when his endeavors outgrew the house, we decided not to invest in another property, commercial or residential, in Oregon. There were many superficial reasons we could list for why Oregon was no longer home to us: taxes were high, crime rates were on the rise, owning or developing the farmland we had dreamed of settling into was cost-prohibitive, etc. Yet, as I recall, the state of Oregon never really felt like home to either of us, for reasons we wouldn't understand until we had left it behind. Needless to say, that house near Gresham was not a skillet-hanger.

We put the real estate we owned up for sale and these properties sold quickly. I had researched land all over the United States, and was most impressed by what Missouri had to offer. So, I took a plane to Springfield and drove around with property agents for five days straight looking for a place that would appeal to what I thought Tom and I would want.

Missouri immediately felt like home to me. Complete strangers waved at me when I drove by, and when they greeted me in person, they didn't speak to me as if their guard was up. The people had a happy and carefree countenance that is hard to describe. The stores and shops were largely Ma and Pa settings instead of the corporate feel dominating the West Coast. Everywhere I went had a strange, underlying "back-home" sense about it, like I had traveled into an episode of *The Andy Griffith Show* or *Mayberry R.F.D.* Having come from pine tree territory as a child and then hailing later from the land of deserts, I had only seen Missouri landscaping twice during trips for ministry training. Most of my familiarity with this stunning land was through magazines, postcards, and calendars, but as I was riding over the hills of this new state for the first time as a potential resident, I felt something I had never felt before as I observed the farmland and bur oak shade trees that decorated the earth around me.

I was _home_. This was skillet terrain for sure!

One of the farmhouses we visited immediately struck a chord in my spirit. It sat atop a thirteen-acre parcel with oak trees all along the back of the property. Just outside the house was a big, red, timber-built barn with white trim, the spitting image of that classic Old MacDonald setup with massive swinging doors and a wooden slide latch. The barn hadn't housed animals for years, and when I first saw it, I noted that it was in need of some sprucing up, but the construction was solid. Once inside, I noticed small details others might miss: The trim around each window and doorway was thick and heavy, installed before the cheap, flimsy stuff had become the norm; the layout of the rooms wasn't modern, rather, it formed a sort of circle with the living room at the center, suggesting that the home had been built room by room as the owner could afford it, with a hub of family gatherings as top priority. Although it looked like it had been lived in, it was clear from the first room to the last that it had been well cared for. The listing price was incredibly affordable as well, considering that this kind of land back in Oregon would go for well over a million dollars. The cost of living in Missouri was already showing its true and blessed colors, and the home was listed for much less than a quarter of what it would have gone for on the West Coast.

My daughter had accompanied me on the trip with her husband, and I had asked him to inspect the old farm house. He had worked with us at the camp and had inspected many buildings during that seven year stretch. Once he gave the nod of approval, I called Tom and described the house and, after a few days of contemplation and phone communication with him and other inspectors, Tom encouraged me to make an offer, so I did.

As history will tell, the offer was accepted. Tom and I wrapped up all our loose ends in Oregon and made what I had hoped to be our final "hang-my-skillet" move.

Our children, Joe, Allie, and Donna, all had little reason to remain in Oregon as well, so within a short time, our entire clan was stationed within only miles of each other in a new state with new possibilities. I was happier than I had ever been. I had all my kids and grandkids nearby, living in a nice little town full of kind people. I loved that home more than any place I had lived, and in its own warm, inviting, country way, it loved on me right back.

The first time I mentioned the skillet-hanging ceremony after our move to the farmhouse, it was welcomed with great support from my family. I just needed to take care of a few things first. Our ministries had to be up and running. Boxes shut tight for half my adult life had to be opened and the sentimental contents within finally hung or placed within view and enjoyed. My kids and their immediate families had to all be available for a gathering. Oh, and one of the most important pieces of the puzzle…*a horse*. I had to have a horse!

Once I had the horse of my dreams, then the house of my dreams could be appropriately christened with my favorite skillet on a hook.

Allie, Joe, and Donna (who was married by this time) were all grown with lives of their own, and it was no longer my priority to ensure they were bathed, fed, properly schooled, or mothered. Sundance had taught me that in order to fully enjoy a horse friend, I would have to have immediate priorities taken care of first, and now I could cross that off my list. The home where I had tried to hang my skillet back in Salem,

Oregon, didn't have room for a horse, and this Missouri land had room for a whole herd of them, so making space for them was another item I could mark as done. Our ministries had never slowed, but because I had all of my attention to devote to them now, I found myself with free time during the day to spend on a hobby, so that, also, was no longer a major concern.

I felt it in my spirit.

I had been drawn to the house.

I had been drawn to the barn.

I had been drawn to the community.

I had been drawn to this life that was now preparing the way for me to step into the lifelong equestrian vision.

I had been drawn to a dream of owning horses from my earliest memory, and God hadn't yet allowed that dream to fizzle in my heart, despite all the curveballs that had been thrown at me.

It was happening. *Finally* happening.

And now, it was just a matter of finding the perfect horse…or two! Then we would find the perfect resting place for the skillet.

Among the first horses I brought back to the farm was this absolutely gorgeous black fox trotter, smooth as silk, standing fifteen hands high. She looked just like the stallion from the movie *Black Beauty*, except female. Missouri Fox Trotters are known for their smooth ride, and since Tom had now developed arthritis in all his major joints, it seemed the perfect match for him. For myself, I bought a buckskin Quarter Horse, slightly smaller than Tom's.

The day came when Tom and I would ride together again for the first time in *years*! Saddling them up and readying them for the adventure was just as exciting as the first time. My heart sped as I slipped my foot into the stirrup and swung my other leg onto my new friend's back.

I breathed in deeply the air of satisfaction. I patted the trail horse's neck and grabbed the reins with elated anticipation, directing him to the edge of the path on our land. And when we were ready, Tom and I looked at each other, smiled, and kicked—ever so slightly—propelling the horses forward and onward to our castle in the sky. Just like our ride through the mud pit, this would be a historical day in our lives.

But there was one minor detail I could not have seen coming.

It was almost humorous at first, as we immediately noticed the pace of rhythm between our horses. Tom's horse, a "trotter," was trotting at the gait that it had been bred and trained to do. My horse, a "trail" horse, was walking, as it also had been bred and trained to do. Tom tried to slow his mare down a little, but she didn't exactly appreciate being forced to move slower than was natural for her, so I nudged mine to keep up with Tom. He cooperated with my request for only a minute, and then began to challenge me by "crop-hopping," a term referring to when a horse issues a warning-level bucking out of irritation. I was not ready for that. In fact, it unnerved me. It had been years since I had ridden, and I was sorely out of practice. We both were. So, once again, Tom attempted to slow his mare down to match the speed of my mount.

This went on for a while, and the race announcer commentary of our pathetic little dance might have sounded something like this:

Aaaaand, they're off! Miss Persnickety Trotter had a bit of an awkward start, but now she and Tom are rounding up ahead as they move in for the first turn! On the far outside, Captain Casual Trails and Nita are attempting to gain back some of the ground lost by his tardy takeoff... Nita's closing in on the pass! Ohhh! Captain Casual Trails is pulling in for the lead! Bet you didn't expect that, folks! Not to worry! Not to worry! Here comes Tom on the turn-around! Miss Persnickety Trotter is heading back to battle it out with the leader ladies and gentlemen, paving the way for the back stretch...

Captain Casual Trails appears to be happy in second place, traveling through a quarter of eighty-three and two-fourths seconds behind... Passing the half-mile pole, Miss Persnickety Trotter is slowing down again, closing the distance by only a length and a half. This could be anyone's race, folks!... Approaching the quarter pole, Captain Casual Trails pulls into the lead and takes center of the track! But Miss Persnickety Trotter won't take this lying down, people! Look at her go! She's closing in on the final stretch! Will either of these horses make up their mind!?

Miss Persnickety Trotter *did* take this lying down, in a matter of speaking...

It would have likely continued to be amusing if the ride had lasted long enough for the four of us to develop an agreeable tempo to our movements, especially since these horses were not used to their handlers *or* to having been ridden side by side, and it was feasible that it could eventually all be worked out. Alas, our little adventure was cut short when Tom's mare got downright frustrated. She dropped to the ground and started rolling around with Tom still in the saddle.

Tom barely removed himself before being rolled on by his horse, and *thankfully* he was not hurt, but his confidence in our little escapade was nearly gone. When he tried to remount, the mare continued her protest by crop-hopping him forward and over her neck. He flew, landing on the ground in front of her large flaring nostrils.

"Nah," he said standing up and brushing the dirt and grass from his trousers. "I'm not doin' this."

I didn't blame him for a second. These horses may have been great for other riders on another farm somewhere, but the chemistry wasn't jiving for us. And after learning through Sundance what could transpire if I held onto a horse when it wasn't meant to be, I just shrugged and headed back to the barn, knowing even before I got there that the fox trotter had to be re-homed and replaced by another Captain Casual Trails.

The lady who bought Tom's horse had a couple of her own, one of which she offered to trade straight across for Tom's mare. It was a trail horse like mine. When I had gone to see him in person, his temperament had been the major selling point. His owner went on and on about how gentle he was. How kind, how amiable, how delightful, how "anyone could ride him," how he was "just the sweetest thing"…all the syrupy things one wants to hear before committing to buy. Joe and his family had gone with me to meet this mild-mannered gelding, and Joe drove me home a few minutes later after I had been bucked to the ground and landed hard on my back, only a foot away from a mangled garbage pile containing sharp shards of glass and metal scraps. It was a real rodeo show, one that did me in for a while.

I was laid up for weeks.

Needless to say, the horse was not all he had been advertised to be, and the owner sincerely felt awful. She seemed truly as shocked by this horse's behavior as I was.

I wanted to believe that this was just an unusual coincidence—not a sign or warning from anyplace divine—but I had a hard time completely letting go of my reservations. First, a potentially dangerous riding session watching Tom bite the dust; then, getting nearly bucked from a "gentle" trail horse, myself. It wasn't looking good.

That old, familiar "gut feeling" had started to toy with my heartstrings again.

I knew that there was enough good reason to believe that this time around would be different, merely by how strongly I had felt drawn to a state and property so ripe with opportunity to finally embrace the horse fantasy. So, after numerous painful therapy visits to the chiropractor, I set out on my search again, even before my body had completely healed.

"Old Man" was the next to join our family. He was an old retired roping horse, and he was the most promising of all. Joe, Donna, Donna's husband James, and Tom had all had a turn riding him. I even took my baby granddaughter for a short spin around the barnyard on him, and he did very well. Old Man seemed to be more suitable than some of the others. I personally couldn't bring myself to ride more than just a circle or two around the barn. I wanted to, I thought about it, I fantasized about it all the time, but every opportunity I had was fraught with growing trepidation. Being a novice rider, and *way* out of practice, you can't safely ride a horse the way you should unless you are willing to climb atop the saddle and spend time learning how they move, practicing your commands, and letting them become familiar with your personality. But I couldn't get on that saddle for any real length of time as long as my gut was telling me not to. My body was still weak and aching, but more than anything, my confidence was greatly shaken from the last horse that bucked me off. Another fall could have only made things worse, in all ways.

Nevertheless, I continued to add to the herd, in hopes that Tom and I would someday be able to saddle up with Joe, Allie, Donna, and their spouses. Soon, I had five full-sized horses on my land. But in the interest of including my grandkids in the excitement, I thought it would be fun to get something smaller, less intimidating for them, so I also bought a pregnant miniature mare we named "Little Mama."

My purchase of the mini wasn't a big deal. I hadn't even thought for a moment that I would ever seriously invest in more than one. On one of my birthdays years prior, Tom had taken me to the state fair, where he and I saw a miniature horse for the first time. (Mind you, I am not talking about a pony. Miniature horses are tiny horses. Ponies are larger than miniature horses and are a completely different breed altogether.) When I saw the miniature horses at the fair, I was wowed by how adorable they were standing there in that arena competing with other contestants and interacting with all the children. So when we purchased Little Mama, I was sure she was the perfect pet for the grandkids to scratch on. *My* dream had always been to ride off into the sunset with the wind in my hair, but that dream was throwing complications my way at every turn.

As luck would have it, one of my mares had pushed Old Man into the barbed-wire fence and caused a significant lesion on his chest. This happened early one Sunday morning, and even though my veterinarian came out as quickly as she could get there, by the time she arrived, the wound had been open long enough that we could not stitch it up. I had to learn to keep it clean myself. Several times daily I would need to wash and medicate the gaping wound so it could heal without infection.

My confidence in being a horse owner was already—and once again—waning. It was turning into a Sundance deal all over again, but with different circumstances. And then, just like with Sundance, the final blow arrived.

One day, while I was out at the barn feeding the horses some grain and trying to psych myself into believing this horse fantasy was coming true, I began medicating Old Man's chest. The cut appeared clean and showed sign of improvement, which was encouraging. After putting him through what I am sure must have been an exceptionally uncomfortable ordeal, I walked around to his side to pick up his curry comb. Suddenly, he turned his hind quarters toward me and kicked. Had he wanted to, he could have hurt me badly. As it was, Old Man only used a fraction of the force his powerful leg could have produced, and even though the kick hurt, it was only enough of a warning kick to leave a bruise. But my leg was not the only place that felt the sting. The trust between horse and rider was also severely tainted. I was thankful it hadn't been worse, but as far as what that kick did to my hopes and aspirations, the damage was done.

I walked up to his face, shook my head in anger, and said, "Dumb horse! Why did you do that? Why did you kick me? I was only helping you! Now you've done it. Now I have to get rid of you!" I could no longer trust that horse around me (and especially not around any grandkid of mine), so he had to go.

Later, I was lying on my couch, my body in pain all over, feeling like a little whipped puppy dog. It had only been a short time since I had brought these animals back into my life when Tom had been thrown, I had been bucked off, and now I had been kicked.

How could this be happening?! *Why* was this happening?!

For a while I remained still, wrestling with my thoughts, considering the evidence I had been given. My kids were grown, that much was true, but so was I, and even I was capable of being hurt or possibly killed if even one thing went wrong. How were these other horse owners doing it? How did all these other lucky people have farms and ranches full of these creatures and live to see the day they could simply be enjoyed and not feared? Was *I* the problem? Or was I just bringing home the wrong animals? If it was meant for me to see my dreams come to fruition, what was I doing wrong? And if it wasn't meant to be, why *on earth* was I still pining for the day I would get to experience that joy?

Would it be too much to ask the horsie world to throw me a bone, and spare me from another lemon? I began reevaluating the reason I owned these horses in the first place.

I had been struggling with discouragement for weeks before that kick, and I couldn't drown the memory of that young, comatose girl in the hospital as a child. At the camping facility in Oregon, I had been through a great deal of safety instruction, had been certified for high-ropes courses, and had observed the lifeguard training for our pool. The educational material spoke in depth about the dangers of one shallow-end dive or one slip near the pool's edge. I watched as one mock victim after another (fellow lifeguards in training) were pulled from the waters during their training sessions. The lifeguards had to head out to the deep end to retrieve a face-down, motionless swimmer, position their hands and forearms around the victim's chest and chin to stabilize the spine, perform a turn to bring the victim's airways to the surface of the water, and then swim the victim to the shallow end. From there, the life-guards had to walk their body around in circles until assistant lifeguards brought the stabilizing gurney. Then, the lifeguards would use red foam blocks to steady the victim's head, strap him or her down, and then lift the victim from the waters and practice waiting for Emergency Medi-cal Services to arrive. While all of this was underway, and assuming the victim in the rescue scenario was cognitive, the rescuers had to rehearse speaking with him or her and trying to keep the person awake. Our life-guard trainer was qualified and professional. He made *sure* that everyone at the camp—whether training to be a lifeguard or not—understood the risks involved in pool play. At the same time, of course, I had to become CPR certified, which involved another whole list of risk assessment and rescue intervention skills. (The CPR classes in those years were far more intense and educational than they are today.) By the time the staff members walked away with their lifeguard certificates, the lot of us had been submerged for months in a mentality that respected a frightening reality: One false move can, and sometimes does, end a life.

Safety, safety, safety. Thanks to my days in camping, I was positively saturated with thoughts of safety.

The risks introduced by horses were, even here in Missouri with the best land and my family all grown, too high to keep justifying the addition of more geldings and mares to my property.

So there, that day, alone in my living room, amongst a pile of horse-wound heating pads, ice packs, and chiropractor bills, and with every muscle and joint throbbing like an old, *old* woman, I finally did the unthinkable.

I gave up.

I felt tears swell up in my eyes and said, "Lord, I'm way too young to feel this old. This isn't what I've dreamed of my whole life, and I'm done. Every time I try to make the desires of my heart come to pass, I am met with a resistance that I can no longer ignore. I have to simply believe that even if this horse thing was to be *my* will, it is clearly not yours. To that end, I will be obedient."

And with that, I felt the equine dream had been short lived, but I began making plans to re-home every horse I owned…

Except for Little Mama. She could stay.

Little Mama was harmless.

But…if Little Mama is safe, I wondered…

I can't say that it came as a sudden epiphany. It was more of a slow and gradual transition, but I started revisiting the driving motives behind my fantasies. I began to look back on all those moments in life when I felt drawn to these animals, and really reflect on what it was that I wanted all those years. Of course there was the adventure, the riding off into the sunset, the romance, the thrill of it all… But above and beyond that, there was a companionship. I never needed to impress a horse with fancy words, and that had never been my skill. These horses were always unassuming and connected with me in ways humans never could. Sure, some people find that same connection with a canine, but the horse had always been at the center of my wiring for as long as I can remember.

Was it possible, then, that the *dream* was right, but the *concept* was wrong?

I know this may appear at first to be a complicated question, but thanks to the world of books and cinema, others have gone before me to ask—and answer—the same question.

When little orphan Annie grew up in a home for girls under the irresponsible and cruel supervision of Miss Hannigan, the thought of finding her true parents haunted her at every waking moment. The dream of locating Mommy and Daddy carried her through one terrible nightmare in her reality to the next, and she never gave up hope. Then, one day, for the sake of public relations, she was fostered by a rich and calloused man by the name of Mr. Warbucks. Not for a moment was Annie considering that this new foster parent would replace her need for her biological mother and father, nor did Warbucks seem for a second to be interested in bonding with her. But, there was the thrill of make believe! The excitement of leaving the girls' home and living in a huge mansion rich with any material item she could possibly ask for, and pretending, even for a while, that she belonged to someone, gave her a taste of life like she'd never had. A part of a family. A child going even one step farther away from an orphanage and closer to finding her real parents.

As the story unfolds, Daddy Warbucks begins to care about Annie, and upon hearing her wish to find her true parents, he puts out a broadcast all over the nation offering a cash reward to anyone who can give any leads on where Annie's real parents are. Annie, through a convoluted journey involving dangers and villains abounding, discovers that her parents had died in a fire when she was a baby; she had spent all this time trailing after ghosts! Warbucks proposes to his secretary and, after saving Annie's life and showering the utmost paternal protection over her while on her quest for her birth parents, asks Annie if she would like to be adopted and move into his home for good. She agrees, and the final scene of the movie is a tear-jerker wherein the little orphan finally has a family to call her own.

In the end, the question answers itself. Annie's dream of finding her parents was spot-on. Finding parents was meant to be. Her *concept* of who those parents would be was skewed by the intensity of her focus. She kept envisioning a sweet little house with a white picket fence, Mama brewing coffee, Daddy reading the paper, and Annie being a part of the biological family who had mistakenly given her away, but who now regretted it and welcomed her back with open arms. When she was handed the happy ending she had always pined for, it was precisely what she wanted, *precisely what she needed,* but it came in the package of Daddy Warbucks, a man she couldn't even see as a fatherly figure until her vision was cleared by letting go of the biological-parents concept.

When I was in my teens, I thought I wanted to be a Hippie-type folk singer. I have no idea where I got it, but I managed to get my hands on a box guitar that I strapped around my back and for a time, I walked around with that thing everywhere. I saw others wandering around with their guitars strapped on, and I wanted to be involved in music, so I just did like other musicians did. Lots of young people played the guitar, so clearly, the guitar was a dream of mine. Right? Not to mention it was much easier strapping a guitar to my back than a set of drums.

I learned how to play the chords, and I guess I wasn't a bad vocalist, but soon, the guitar was uncomfortable, clunky, and hard to wear, and trying to work my clumsy fingers over the strings wasn't natural. When I realized it had become more about an image I was trying to maintain and less about what I could actually offer as a musician, I got over that phase just as quickly as I had started it. But I can reflect on those days now and see where my focus had been skewed. I *dreamed* of being be a guitarist and folk singer, and the dream was spot on! I actually had a lot to offer in the musical sphere, as I am still playing today. However, the *concept* was a guitar, because the only other instrument I had dabbled with were drums, and drums are not something you can strap on your back and make music with. I did not know until my skills were later sharpened that my greatest talent is behind the drum set. By reevaluating my concept from the guitar back to the drums, I found that I had so much more to give the world of music, and I was much more confident. A more natural wiring for me is to keep time. My stint with the guitar was merely a stepping stone, a tasting of the romantic idea that allowed me to hone into what I had been meant to do: stick to drumming.

Was my lifelong dream of galloping off into the wild blue with a full-size horse and half a dozen family members merely a skewed concept? Had I, like Annie, been focused so long on what I thought the package would look like that my vision was blurred to what the dream was actually leading me to? Had I, like my younger, musical self, focused on the more accessible horse instrument that everyone else played while the drum set of the miniature horse world was waiting for me to find harmony in the beat?

Once this notion finally hit home, I prayed and spoke with Tom regarding the possibilities of beginning a miniature horse ranch. "Saddle Horn Ranch," we called it, a clever play on words involving both a literal saddle horn and our last name, and we were excited about all the possibilities. I could still have my equine reality, just downsized a bit...literally. I couldn't ride them, obviously, but my tiny grandkids could do so safely, and just think of all the directions I could take this! I could train them to pull carts! I could show them at horse shows and bring home the ribbons! I could march them in parades! I could love on them and tell them all my secrets and never again fear the inevitable bucking of a disagreeable ride! That was the winning ticket right there!

DING-DING-DING!

The light went on, and my mind raced with newfound determination. My heart leapt with new direction! I did not have to say farewell to the equine life!

I was heading down the right road this time for sure. The dream was still present, but the concept just needed a slight adjustment.

There is more to the story in the coming pages regarding the role that miniature horses played in reforming me as an individual. But what of the skillet?

As mentioned previously, my home burned to the ground as a result of outdated building codes and old wiring, and it was just after the announcement that I had finally found my forever home that the flames took everything—including my favorite, reliable old skillet.

It seemed, more the day of the fire than ever before, that I would never be allowed to settle.

But my story continues.

My mold develops further.

Through the clanging of my skillets on the day they fell, I realized that God would choose my forever home, not me. And through the lesson of the five big horses and one big injury, I had learned that whereas my concept of settling was in a home I had felt called to, it was merely a pit stop toward the home on earth that God was preparing for me. Saddle Horn Ranch was a fun idea, but a hobby farm was not meant to be. I was merely at only one of the crescendos in my waltz, and my life was about to take the most important turn of all.

I believe today that I am currently in my forever home, and I do plan to hang my skillet soon, but when I do, it will be carefully, and with the utmost respect to whatever direction God plans to take me next…And, I will *certainly* ask Him before I attempt to do it!

The lesson of five big horses and one big injury helped me to revise my concepts. Remember to have an open mind when you dream. The package containing your dream may arrive on your doorstep earlier or later than you thought it was due, and it might look different than the one you thought you ordered.

9

Whispers

*T*he auction chant is the sound that sells. When people arrive at an auction, they are mesmerized by the reverberating sounds of auctioneers belting out that fast-paced gibberish cattle-cry intermingled with, "Twenty dollar bid, now thirty, now thirty, will ya gimme forty? Forty dollar bid, now fifty, now fifty, who'll give me sixty?" As the bidder cards pop up all around, each interested bidder feels the adrenaline rush of the moment, knowing that if he or she doesn't act quickly, someone else will go home with the prize. The speed of the atmosphere is hypnotizing, and bidders can return home with more than they ever bargained for as a result of being caught up in the moment.

Nita, having been raised around auction houses, was more than used to this, she knew the drill, and she usually wasn't swayed by the excitement. Today, she had come here to buy, certainly, but she wouldn't be led by an emotional high or taken for a fool.

As she walked the paths through and around the auction yard, Nita heard the voices calling out the various animals up for bid. The donkeys were up for bid now, which meant the miniature horses would be next. The moment was getting closer.

Rounding the corner, she caught sight of the painted ponies she had come here to see, and among them were several other miniature horses stalled and ready for the bid. One man stood on-site to answer questions pertaining to an upcoming auction for four remaining mini horses in what had been a six-horse hitch: horses trained and ready to drive parallel to each other. A feat like that spoke of elevated level of training for sure.

Nita asked the auctioneer about the terms of the sale.

"It's a 'times-the-money,' Ma'am. 'Buyer take their pick,'" the auctioneer said.

Nita understood well what that meant: The highest bidder would be allowed to pick which of the horses he or she wanted from the entire lot, and the dollar amount would be multiplied by the number of horses the winner chose to keep. It was a way for sellers to guarantee the most money for each animal, as well as a way for buyers to walk away with exactly what they wanted.

Thanking the auctioneer, Nita turned to the owner.

"Are these horses registered?"

"No, ma'am. But they're perfect'n every other way. Very agreeable personalities. Workable, obedient, well-trained. Cart-broke, too. Easy to catch!"

Nita had heard a ripe rouse from a seller before, and ended up bucked from the wild thing moments into her first test ride. The result had been a painful recovery. She wasn't planning to swallow the pitch hook, line, and sinker without a proper questioning first. Her puppy, Ducky, had died as a result of a horse running from capture, so that seemed a good place to start.

"Easy to catch?" Nita prompted.

"Oh yeah, sure thing. No problem at all. Jist git yerself a bucket-a grain and they'll come right to ya, jist like a puppy dog."

"That's good to hear. Are they solid? Are they easily spooked?"

"Oh, not at all. They're not afraid-a nothin'. They're parade horses, the lot of them. Used to bein' around a lotta big noises and people throwin' candy, ya know. Nothin' spooks these guys. They're very road savvy. Ready to go! Just what you need!"

"What about shots?"

"Yes, ma'am. Everything's up-to-date."

Nita's eyes fell back on the two perfectly matching, multi-colored paints that had brought her to the auction. Standing at the same height of thirty-two inches at the withers, they were an ideal salt-and-pepper set. A gelding and a mare.

"Are these two related?"

"Nope. Just look-alikes."

"How long have you had them?"

"This filly's been ours since birth. She's ten years old now. Th'other came to our place about a year ago, and he's about six."

"Has she ever been bred?" Nita gestured to the female.

"Yeah, she's given us a few babies now, all of 'em healthy. No issues with that."

Nita was feeling pretty good about the information so far. He seemed the honest type.

"You said they're pretty easy to manage?"

The owner smiled, nodded, and laughed. "Easiest in the bunch! These here are my lead hitch in a team of six. Excellent drivers. They know what they're doin'. Bid with confidence, ma'am."

As another interested buyer appeared with questions and the auctioneer was gearing up for the bid to start, Nita offered a quick thanks and retreated, taking her place in the crowd, bidder card ready.

I won the bid that day. At $375, "times the money" for two horses, buyer's choice, I took the lead drivers home for $750. I also asked for the previous owner's number in case I had questions later on, and he was happy to oblige. He encouraged me to call any time.

I was very excited to get the horses home and see what such wonderful minis were capable of on my own land. I had named them before I could get them home. By this time, I had already accumulated a few other minis around the property, so the newbies would have other bodies to warm up to.

The first night was thrilling. I unloaded them into their stalls, spoke to them as usual, and made sure they were spoiled with as much grain and hay as they could possibly want as a welcome-home gift. I noticed that Tink (short for "Tinker Bell"), the female driver, didn't want me to touch her, as was clear by the whipping of her head each time I tried, but I was sure she would warm up to me. Tonka, the gelding, didn't seem ecstatic about being handled either, but it was the first night in their new home, and I just figured it would take time.

Boy, they were a sharp looking pair! A quintessential Christmas-card duo, the likes of which would make such a profound impression on the universe that the song would have to be rewritten to say, "Dashing through the snow, in a two-miniature-horse cart."

As soon as my schedule allowed, I bounded to the barn, harnesses in tow, with a smile from ear to ear. On the inside, I was leaping for joy, determined that the distant behavior I noticed the night they were brought home was a fluke. Some kind of retaliation against all the hub-bub they had been put through in the last week. Considering they had been driven seven or eight hours from their previous home in a neigh-boring state all the way to the local auction, penned up for several days in a cramped setting with bizarre cattle smells and an unfamiliar food routine, and *then* forced into my trailer and hauled to a new home, I had reason to believe it was just a natural occurrence.

It would be fine. They had been given a few days to settle in, prance freely about the corral, and graze at their leisure, so I was sure they were up for a circle about the yard pulling their carts.

Using a grain bucket as a lure, I set out into the corral and made the stereotypical click-calls. When neither of them came to me, I wandered farther in. Both Tink and Tonka made every attempt to trot off in what-ever direction was opposite of where I stood.

Odd.

Perhaps they just needed more time. That's it… Just give them a couple more days…

After a while of wandering around, frustration beginning to set in, I managed to earn Tonka's trust—or, rather, his interest in the grain bucket—long enough to slip the lead rope around his neck. From there, I tied him to the fence and went in again after Tink. Around and around I walked, and finally, I sped up out of desperation. She wasn't inter-ested in being anywhere near me, and all the come-hither tricks in the book were a no-go. Nothing doing. No grain, no goodies, nothing. She wanted absolutely nada to do with the likes of me.

The next day was the same, and the day after that, and the day after that…

A couple of weeks passed, and I was starting to think there was more to the story of Tink and Tonka than the man at the auction had told me.

I thought long and hard about the behavior I was observing, but *parade horses*! That term in and of itself spoke of animals that were not only used to, but thrived in, an atmosphere of interaction.

I woke up one morning determined. I decided that whether Tink liked it or not, she was going to be caught and harnessed. Once she had been through it a few times with me, a caring nurturer of horsekind, she would see that I meant her no harm.

The wrangling started off as any other day had, with clicking, calm tones of speech and roping Tonka out of the way. As I honed in on Tink, it was the usual game of evasion. Finally, I managed to edge her into the barn where she fled to a stall. No longer given the same room as she'd had in the outside corral, I knew I had her. Closing in a little at first, she panicked and set out to pass me. I whipped my hands in the air like a wide bear-hug, cornering her in. Each time she tried to escape, I inched closer, arms wide, like a stall door on legs, ever drawing nearer. She flailed about for what seemed like an eternity, and each time she did, I held my ground, firmly gripping my limbs about her and releasing again when she backed off.

If I had known the wrestling match was going to be so wild, I wouldn't have taken the risk. A miniature horse, though not the same level of danger as a full-sized horse, was certainly capable of hurting me if she had such an intention. But as the seconds flew and my willpower swelled, I figured I had started something that I needed to finish. If nothing else, this horse was *going to* see that I meant her no harm, even if I had to endure a bruise or two in the process.

I kept thinking to myself, *What is the deal with this horse?! For cryin' in a bucket, she's a parade horse! She's supposedly used to being caught, haltered, and made to walk amongst loud sounds and tons of people in a six-horse hitch! What the heck is wrong with her? Does she not like me for some reason? Do I scare her? Or is she just being a stinker?*

By the time I finally had her successfully pinned and slipped the rope around her neck, I was far more shocked and dismayed at the whole ordeal than I was proud of myself for proving anything to her. Standing there, looking at this horse who had been forcibly worn down, I saw something I had not only never seen with my own two eyes, I had never even *heard* of it.

Nita working with Tink.

Tink was shaking. Positively *trembling* in fear. Her eyes were as wide as the Missouri River, ears back, tail tucked. Every muscle in her body was shuddering…and there *I* was, standing there as the new lady who wanted to show love and friendship, scaring the living daylights out of her. Not at all what I had in mind for this little mare.

What was all this? I was the *horse whisperer* for crying out loud! I was the companion of the equine world, not the enemy. Usually when I whispered to my four-legged friends, they listened. But Tink was acting as if she had just lost a head-on match with a grizzly bear.

I felt bad for her. It was such a heartbreaking sight, watching her shuddering there in a corner like a beaten doe. But what else could I have done? I truly had been ever so patient for days, and I knew that when horses are allowed to roam free without a handler, the resistance they put up frequently only worsens, so I had captured her in the only way I knew how at that time. And even when I was firm with her, I was gentle in the process. So, why was she afraid of me?

At least I had caught her, and now I could stand beside her for a while, allowing her to observe that I was the best friend she would ever have, *if* she would have me. However, this catching method was most definitely *not* going to be the norm.

I eventually returned to the house, located the number to the previous owner from the auction, and dialed. When he answered, I was relieved.

"Hey, I'm glad you answered! It's Nita, the buyer of your two lead mini drivers at the auction a couple of weeks ago."

"Oh yeah, hi!" the voice on the line rang out. "How's it goin'?"

"Well, I'm sure you're busy, so I will get straight to the point," I said. I wanted to keep it short, so as not to give this man the impression that I would be a needy new owner with plans to call every five minutes with questions. "The horses aren't exactly settling in the way I had hoped. Both of them are very hard for me to catch. I can kinda get Tonka to cooperate with me once in a while, but Tink… I can't figure her out. I had to pin her to the corner of the stall just now and when I finally had her caught—"

"Oh, sure," he interrupted. "Yeah, I can help ya out."

For a moment, I was relieved that he was about to share the secret to interacting with her…but then, I found myself stunned!

"What ya gotta do is, ya jist get a bucket, coax her into a stall, corner her in, slip the rope around her neck and if she doesn't do what ya want, ya jist take the rope and beat her with it until she behaves. Don't worry. She'll listen to ya then. Easy as puddin'."

Was this guy serious?

The absence of a follow-up laugh was all the evidence I needed to establish that he was, in fact, instructing me to—beat—the horse…with a *rope*!

My response was immediate. My tone was matter-of-fact, but not provoking.

"Okay, well, thank you. That was all I needed to know."

The indifference behind his tone of voice when he instructed me to beat her was enough evidence to me that he was already so immersed in his ways of thinking that it was a lost cause to attempt converting him into a more caring handler. I knew beyond any shadow of any doubt that this man—this oh-so-casual beater of horses—wasn't going to change what he was doing based on the thoughts that were flying through my head had I decided to share them, so I merely let him go.

And I *never* called him again. *Ever.*

I had, as so many others had been before me, brought home more from the auction than I bargained for after all.

To be honest, when I observed Tink shaking the way she did in that stall, the thought had crossed my mind that she may have been abused at some point, but I couldn't have assumed that was the case—nor could I have assumed the man from the auction had been capable of it. And for that matter, even if I secretly believed that he had beaten her, I figured he surely wouldn't admit it, so possibly by calling him for advice, he would be able to give me tips on an alternate method of catching her.

But he *did* admit to beating her. Quite openly in fact. And that exposed a truth that made my skin crawl: If he was willing to admit so nonchalantly to beating her with a rope in order to catch her, what other methods of rough horse handling might he have done to her that he wasn't telling me?…

Tonka had no doubt been placed in this man's care as well, but it had been revealed to me that day at the auction that he had owned Tink since birth, and Tonka was only at his farm for about a year, which explained why Tonka was somewhat more trusting toward me.

I was infuriated.

And then I thought of how Tink looked in that stall.

My heart broke.

There I had stood, looking at her, wondering what was wrong with this troubled animal, and only now was it occurring to me that she was only cowering because she had been trained to anticipate a beating.

My gut wrenched with sorrow at the memory of that sight. I didn't have any control over the hell she had been through, and that reality fell upon me with great weight that day.

It took a lot of determination and commitment to that horse for me to plod onward in the coming months. I had everything that horse could ever need, including love, and all I received from her were frightened sideways glances and retreat. She wanted nothing to do with me.

Day after day, I got my bucket of grain and headed to the fields and the corral, rattling Tink's grain, whistling cheerfully, clicking a happy greeting, speaking in calm tones…but day after day, she ran from me like a battered foal from a predator. I watched training videos, tried this method, then tried that, searched the Internet, looked in books, all to no avail. It felt like the more time I spent trying to bond with her, the more she feared me. At every turn, I met another wall.

One day, I finally managed to get her back in the stall where she had no escape. I retrieved her halter, and took a deep breath. Tink had been with me quite a while now, and I had only shown her patience, respect, and compassion since her move from her previous owner's home. Those walls would never begin to chip away if I didn't make my move, and there was no time like the present. So I steadied my nerves and approached her. Again.

The second she saw the halter, she pinned her ears, her muscles tightened and she started running about wildly, as usual. Her tail tucked inward, a sure sign that she was expecting a beating. I fought to maintain my cool, all the while keeping my movement and tone gentle. She fought this way and that, never once kicked at me, but her head whipped up and down, left and right, as her body turned circles in the struggle.

"Easy, Tink… Easy there," I continued.

And still, she wrestled.

I increased my volume only a little, trying with all my might to calm her, love on her, and be her friend.

And still, she wrestled.

Backing away, I let her have time to calm down, spoke to her softly but firmly, and after a minute or two, when she appeared slightly pacified, I inched my way closer to her. Carefully, I considered every part of my body in my approach: soft steps, relaxed posture, amicable and precise motions, like a tender but unyielding adoptive mother over a child with an abusive past.

And still, she wrestled.

At this point, with frustration kicking in to a pinnacle point, I thought perhaps the only way she might warm up to the idea of a halter is if she were to see that neither the halter or myself was going to bite her, rest assured that no rope would fly through the air and strike her, and then, maybe *then*, she would relax. That *alone* would be progress.

With solid resolve—an internal fortitude announcing my horse-whispering purpose toward her—I spoke smoothly one last time.

"Alright, Tink. Here's the deal. I'm not your abuser. I never have been. All I have done is loved you. Now you have to let me harness you at some point or other, despite what others have done to you. I *chose* you, bought you, and paid for you with my own money, because I saw the value in you. I still see value in you, despite all you've been through. You *can* make it through this. If you can't stand still and be haltered or harnessed, your amazing driving abilities can't be used. You may have come from a hard situation, but now you need to realize that you're loved. Do you really want to be stuck in this level of growth? Is that what you want? You're worth so much more than this."

Tink didn't move, apart from a mild shaking, her eyes always watching every move I made as she calculated what direction she would need to go to avoid me.

"Come on, now, Tink. Let's do this. Okay? We can do this. You and me."

I would love telling this part of the story all the more if I could say that my words broke through her damaged concepts of humanity. How happy it would be if my conversation with Tink that day resulted in my slipping the halter over her head without a struggle. Two estranged beings connecting through their first whispering ritual. A momentous breaking down of communication barriers. A historic alliance of man and beast against all odds. Finally friends! Comrades at last! What a victory that would have been!

But that's not what happened.

She fought until the very end, straining against me, never as a means to assert her own authority above me, but out of the deepest fear I've ever seen in a horse. I had heard that an old, tried-and-true method of getting a horse to cooperate was to grip them around the ears and twist them painfully. There was no way in this life or the next I would ever do such a cruel and brutal thing, but judging by how terrified she increasingly became the closer I got to placing the halter over and around her ears, I knew she had probably experienced many ear-tweakings in her lifetime. The more I saw the effects of abuse showing in and through her, the more angered I became at her previous handlers—and the more determined I became to see this harness placed on her head so Tink could see for herself that those days were over.

In the end, I won.

But I didn't feel like a winner.

There she was—*again*—cowering away from me, every muscle uncontrollably shivering in anxiety and panic. So frightened of me that she shook almost convulsively.

A minute later, I flew through the front door of my house in a fit of hysterics and burst into Tom's computer room. He looked up from his work and wrinkled his brow.

"What's wrong?" he asked.

"I've decided I'm done with Tink," I launched immediately. "I don't know what to do with her! Nothing I try works, and I can't do it anymore! I can't do it! I give up! I bought her to be a driving horse, but you can't even get a halter around her head, and when you *do*, she stands there shaking as if she's just been flogged!"

Tom sat, patiently listening, and I could tell from his expression that he was processing the information and weighing potential solutions. He had heard all about my conversation with the previous owner in which I was told Tink was beaten with a rope, so he knew what I was up against.

Having gotten that initial rush of frustration out into the open air, I steadied myself to keep my cool, and then continued.

"I'm out of ideas. I've done everything I have ever known to do for her and she still trembles every time I act like I'm going to use her for what I bought her for…"

Then, a thought suddenly occurred to me, and I blurted it out.

"She's a broken horse. *She's a broken horse!* Full-on. Like a bowling ball dropped on a teacup. Broken! That man beat her to the point she's useless and then disposed of her so she'd be someone else's problem… That's why he was selling his prized driving team."

"Well," Tom said, taking a deep breath and twisting his expression in thought. "That last bit might very well be true, but re-homing her may not be necessary yet."

"What do you mean?"

"What if you were to catch Tonka, tie him up where Tink could see him, brush him down, scratch around his ears, you know…harness *him* up first. Would that do anything if Tink was able to see her buddy out there getting geared up without a big rope beat-down?"

It wasn't that his suggestion wasn't a great idea. It was actually better than any I had thought of myself. But I remained skeptical that there was any progress to be made with Tink.

Heading out to the barn in the following days, I did what Tom had suggested. Tonka was still sometimes a little harder to catch than the other horses, but we were discovering a working system. I slowly reintroduced him to his gear, one piece at a time. Tink appeared to be slightly less nervous about it, but she still didn't want me near her.

Among the growing list of minis I had been accumulating was a cream-colored, spunky little thing we named "Cameo." She was Little Mamma's baby, and from her first day of life forward, I was like a two-legged mother to her. Everywhere I went, she was in my back pocket, so to speak. If other horses got anywhere near me, she would throw off little warning kicks toward them and reestablish her position closest to me. Constantly nuzzling me and loving on me, I found her to be a great comfort during my early days with Tink, as I knew there would at least be one horse on my land that wanted me always by her side. I have found comfort many times with her nearby. She was originally bred to show, but her mama was sold to me while she was still pregnant, and when Cameo was born and displayed signs of developmental stifle disease (a genetic abnormality in the physical relationship between the horse's knee cap, tibia bone, and femur bone, causing the horse to limp), she no longer had value as a show horse. To *me*, however, Cameo would always have limitless value, just because she was my little pal.

One day, I was out caring for the horses and seeing to my daily duties, and here came Cameo, like always, driving up and ahead of all the others for my attention. I greeted her and scratched her head all around her ears. Then I saw Tink a hundred yards or so away watching my every move. I looked at Tink for a minute, and then I looked back at Cameo. Here was this little animal, born with a joint disease, zero value to the equine world for any reason other than companionship, striving daily to be my closest friend. I didn't have a bucket of grain in my hands.

I didn't have a treat. I wasn't bearing gifts of any kind. I was completely empty-handed, with nothing to offer her at that precise moment other than my affection, and that was enough for her.

And then there was Tink.

While my hands were busy doting on Cameo, my eyes were fixed on Tink, and my brain was abruptly bombarded with a flash of reality.

In that instant, I started to really question my understanding of her, and like the Grinch whose heart grew three sizes in one day, my heart inflated toward her. When I looked at Tink again, she appeared suddenly smaller, more vulnerable than she ever had before. More innocent. And there, in that uneventful hour, in her time of grazing, just minding her own business about the yard like horses do, I shook my head in disbelief.

It was like someone removed my blinders, and I was rapidly seeing her for who she was. I gazed long and hard at her, studied her movements, and allowed the moment to speak truth to my consciousness.

"What happened to you, Tink?" I said from a distance. "What are you trying to tell me? What is going on in that memory of yours that you're trying to communicate?"

Tink swished her tail casually, bent her head to the ground, and chomped some grass. To an outsider, she was just a horse acting like a horse, but I knew better. This was merely an intermission. The beatings she had received, the installment of fear, the imprinting of all things harmful and degenerating to healthy outlook and expectations, all of it was merely on pause. It was never gone, it was just suspended until the next time she heard the familiar footsteps of a human.

It wasn't *me* she was afraid of.

It wasn't *me* she wanted to keep her distance from.

It was pain.

Abuse.

I couldn't fully wrap my brain around the epiphany that was occurring at the time, but in only a second of comparing sweet Cameo with troubled Tink, it was like I beheld her for the first time.

Who could do this to you? I thought. *Who would be so calloused? So selfish? How could someone intentionally damage a beautiful little thing like you so irreversibly for the sake of their own narcissistic convenience? How can I be your friend? How can I fix this? Can I fix this? Tell me. What can I do?*

Then and there, I committed myself to loving her. I didn't care if she wasn't the prized mini I thought I was buying that day at the auction.

She and I had something in common…

Her trust had been broken in the past due to a handler who used a rope as a tool to hurt her.

My trust had been broken in the past due to my observation of people's behavior within the ministry and the tragedy that occurred in my early life.

The development of trust was broken.

I was as damaged as she was.

We were both simply *broken*…

The lesson of Tink was not lost on me: I was *not* the "horse whisperer" I thought I had been. Based on our humanized concepts of what the term "horse whisperer" meant, it had been in my head all this time that those gifted with such an ability would find a way of whispering what *they* had on *their* agenda to a horse, and the horse would respond to the handler's whispers. But thanks to the lesson of five big horses and one big injury, I had learned that concepts aren't reliable. Rather, horse whisperers are exactly the opposite of what I had thought. They *listen* and *hear* what the horse is communicating through languages of their own.

In the following days, I committed to learning from the world's leading horse trainers, celebrated individuals who helped me over several years understand how to work with Tink, Tonka, or other horses to use their curiosity to earn their trust. Some of the techniques were so simple, once I understood how to control the horses' feet, require their respect, and help them get past their fears. I still recall the first day Tink finally let me slip a harness around her head without a fight. I went running into my house and, once again, burst into Tom's computer room shouting like a little girl on Christmas morning, "I whispered! I whispered!" He immediately smiled, congratulated me on my update, shared in my happy moment of celebration, and then followed me all the way to the barn to watch me halter her right in front of him. He wanted to see the horse whisperer with his own eyes.

I had done it!

Or, rather, *we* had done it. Tink and me. Together. She had given me a little bit of trust that day. It was the beginning of a new life for her. I could not have broken through to her, had she not wanted to receive it.

The rest of her driving gear came next. The more equipment I attached to her, the more she relaxed under my touch, *embracing the purpose I had for her*. Once she was put under the control of the reins, she drove like a *dream*! Even the tiniest fluctuation of my directive motions achieve a response from her, but it would have never happened if I hadn't stopped being the speaker and opened my senses to be the listener.

A lot can be said of where a person—or an animal—is at mentally when you cross paths.

Thanks to Tink, I had learned something about listening. *Really* listening.

When an ad came up online for another mini that was trained to drive, listed at only two hundred dollars, I headed out to see her immediately. The first time I saw her, I thought about how much she looked just like Coco, the small horse from my childhood. She was standing in a pen with two full-sized horses. The seller made his way into the pen to try to catch her, but she evaded him again and again. He must have run around for fifteen straight minutes in that one small area, pulling every trick in the book, but she wanted nothing to do with him.

It was a Nita-and-Tink scene all over again. The last thing I needed was another hard-to-catch horse. However, either out of curiosity or compassion, I felt compelled to hang in there.

Once he had caught her, after such a trying ordeal, he roped her and walked her around in circles some distance from me.

She was injured, and it was *obvious*, although that little detail had somehow managed to slip his mind when the seller listed her, and again while giving directions on how to find his place.

"Why is she limping like that?" I asked.

The closer the Coco-look-alike got to me, the more apparent it was that her shoulder looked stiff, and she was clearly limping.

"Well, now, a couple of days ago, a bear came through here, spooked all of the horses, and this little one ran straight into the barbed wire. She'll heal up pretty good though, in a few days."

A bear?… Was that the best tale he could weave?

Barbed wire?!

Did I look like a fool to this man?

"Just a second," I said, politely interrupting the pitch he was preparing to give. "If a bear had spooked her into a fence, wouldn't she be all cut up?" My eyes fell to the mare again, and I searched for any sign that the seller's seemingly ridiculous ruse might hold some truth. "A horse doesn't escape a run-in with barbed wire without a scratch, especially a run-in so severe that they come out of it limping on an injured shoulder. There's not a mark on her anywhere…"

"Ain't that somethin'?" he said, completely avoiding my concern.

I had a horse back home with stifle disease. I had seen horses walk with an abnormal gait, and I knew very well this man's story was beyond ridiculous. This horse had been spooked into barbed wire by a bear?

Some people are simply terrible story-weavers.

"Did you call a vet?"

"No," he responded promptly. "But ol' Billy down the road is real good with animals. He took one look at 'er an' said she'd be fine."

"I see."

About this time, the seller's wife appeared with a child. I imagine it was all staged to impress me by showing me how great this mini was with children, but when they hoisted that kid up on that horse's back and let him ride her, it only worsened her limp.

The whole act was preposterous.

I started to thank them and let them know that I wasn't interested in the sale, but the seller's wife helped the child dismount, took the lead rope, and led her out of the pen to stand right next to me. I reached out to touch her, and she flinched…just like Tink.

For a moment, the rest of the world blurred away. I wasn't focused on the seller, his wife, or the child. I leaned in, and listened for a whisper. I opened my senses to hear what she might have been communicating to me in a language with no words.

The horse's eyes were so sad, and yet, I could see that same flicker of fear. There was a tremendous hurt there that I was picking up on. A misery that I wouldn't have ever noticed in years past. But it was a sensation, an impression, a feeling that I had recently witnessed, and the similarities between Tink and this sorrowful little mini were evident.

Gently and slowly, I gripped my fingers around her halter, put my face right up into hers, and spoke to her, right there in front of everyone.

"Why would I take you home with me? I have to be able to manage you, but you won't let me touch you…"

A few seconds passed between us.

I studied her.

I *listened*.

Talk to me, I thought. *What's going on with you?*

Her face, the same horse features any other horse would have, was somehow pleading. She made no movement or sound, but the history of her past she communicated to me in that moment was profound.

I let go of her halter, stood back at the end of the lead rope, and without a word, I turned and calmly walked over to my trailer, opened the door, and stepped in. She followed me, step by step, and then, amazingly, to my complete surprise, she *leapt* into my trailer.

By now, I had seen how some horses respond to trailers. As a general rule, untrained horses see trailers as a huge mouth waiting to swallow them. They have to be properly introduced to the idea of entering such a space over a period of time. Additionally, the jump to a standard trailer for a miniature horse is a greater height from the ground, causing even the more confident minis to hesitate before making a calculated jump. But this little horse courageously followed me into this giant "mouth" without hesitation. None whatsoever. The same horse who, five minutes prior, would not, *could not*, be caught by her usual handler out of fear was now fearless.

She was not the horse I had come to see, and she would never live permanently on my land as a driver. Even if she had potential as a cart horse based on training, whatever was causing her limp had likely taken that opportunity away from her. So the question I had to ask myself was: Would I buy this horse just to save her? Would I spend a hundred dollars to rescue her and find her a better place to live?

"Two hundred dollars, you said?"

"Yes, ma'am."

"She's got a pretty bad limp there. I'll give you a hundred for her." I figured if I shot too low, I was at risk of an immediate rejection.

It was half what they had listed her for, and initially, they haggled, trying to talk me back up closer to the original amount by mentioning a family with children down the road who had already agreed to the asking price. These people must have really thought I was stupid. That lie was easier to spot than the first one had been. Had the latest spin been the truth, they would have *already sold her* to the interested party who agreed to hand over exactly what they wanted. Why would anyone turn down an offer that met the asking price? Another of their absurd tales fell flat.

"Well, if the family down the road is offering you what you asked for, why don't you just sell her to them?" I wasn't rude at all, but I also wasn't the chump they were trying to make of me. Then, I added, "If you sell her to *me*, she will go to a good home."

"Uhhh," the man responded sheepishly. He looked at his wife, who appeared stumped. "You know, honey, I think we ought-ta jist do the deal. I think that would be a good idea."

I agreed.

Before I even returned home, I had given her a name that honored the horse from my past whom she most resembled: Cocoa Puff. (I added the "Puff" to the name because she was a mare and my original Coco was a gelding. "Puff" seemed more girlish.)

The very first thing I sought to do was have her examined by my vet and farrier. The result was just as I had suspected. Cocoa Puff had *not* recently been in a barbed wire accident. And when I talked about the bear attack, my vet only smiled. That limp had been present, according to the professionals, for months. It had started as some kind of internal joint or shoulder injury, and she had long since healed from whatever the original hurt had been. Physiologically, there was no reason Cocoa Puff should have to limp anymore (aside from muscle atrophy, from which a horse can sometimes be restored through time and physical therapy), but because of her state of mind during healing, she never walked normally after the injury had gone away.

The diagnosis for her suffering was now not only muscular, but mental as well…and debilitating. She had associated the movement and weight upon her leg with something painful. Fixing that became the main goal. And because she had not received the help she should have when she was first injured, her mental state had caused a permanent incapacitation.

I kept her for six months, trying daily to rehabilitate her both physically and mentally. I tried everything from pain meds, to soft leg and shoulder massages, to bending her leg to help her observe the pain was gone. She would not even try putting weight on it. (Perhaps there *was* pain somewhere…?)

When I could see that it was to no avail and that I had done all I could do for her, I listed her as a companion animal only. I was very transparent to those who called that she should never be bred, ridden, or used to pull anything, but that she would make a terrific pet for children and adults alike. When she left, I was happy to see who she was going home with, but the goodbye was heart-wrenching.

Unlike the day I had rescued her from her previous owner, when she sailed into the trailer like Pegasus, as soon as it was time to enter the trailer destined for her new home, she wouldn't go near it. She didn't want to leave my side. It took a lot of calm coaxing, finagling, and one final nudge to get her into that trailer. I could hear her in her own way calling to me, begging me to keep her, and it was *so* sad. I would have regretted making the deal, except I was convinced she was going to a better home. (In fact, I was so at peace with these people, I ended up giving her to them for nothing. She would be one of only two horses, and they were there to find a friend for the one other miniature horse rescue they had waiting at home. Later, they sent me pictures, and I was satisfied that Cocoa Puff would be pampered and loved on more than I could with my then-growing herd of twelve.)

But at the end of the day, I knew something she didn't know: Not *every* horse owner was going to put her through what the last people did. I had done my research, and I had every reason to believe that she would be happy where she was going. To her, I represented the one human that understood and cared for her, and it was that human she was clinging to. Yet, I had bought her to save her, and my work was finished. She was as healthy as she was ever going to be, and I had done my part in accomplishing that, as well as sending her to a place where her usefulness as a "companion only" was precisely what she would be loved for, and nothing else.

Today, Tink is one of the best drivers we have, and she stands as the major turning point for me in communication. Watching that little mare grow taught me something about myself, about others, and about ministry.

It was no longer about showing horses or ribbons.

It was no longer about carts.

It was no longer about parades.

It was no longer about telling them all my secrets.

It was no longer about being the horse whisperer…

It was about listening to the whispers.

Learning when to speak, when to close your mouth, when to be still, when to allow someone else to penetrate your soul with the hurt they carry daily, and when to harness up so you can be used for the purposes you were made for.

I do at times stand in the place of the communicator with these small horses. But just as often, it's the other way around: They talk to me. When words fail.

Experiencing this first-hand, I knew that Saddle Horn Ranch—as clever as that idea had been, and as fun as it would have been to launch a "pretty pony" farm—was no longer the focus. It was a dream that had been drawn when my mold represented a former self, and it no longer embodied what I was being called to do. We would never be the hobby ranch I had envisioned now that this epiphany had struck.

This is the story of how we became "Whispering Ponies Ranch."

Many will come who claim to have the gift, even going as far as to place their fingers on their head and dramatize supernatural revelations. They will move fast, talk the talk, impress others, and have the majority around them convinced of their charismatically proclaimed enlightenment.

But they will miss so much by talking right over the top of that still, small voice ever crying for the listener.

They will miss the *whispers*.

So... What's Your Shape?

There is an old church song called "Change My Heart, Oh God." I have heard this beautiful song all my adult life, and it speaks of such sweet transformation and growth. The lyrics are as follows:

> Change my heart oh God,
> Make it ever true.
> Change my heart oh God,
> May I be like You.
> You are the Potter,
> I am the clay.
> Mold me and make me,
> This is what I pray.

There are several verses in the Bible that this song could have been based upon, the most likely of which is Isaiah 64:8: "But now, O Lord, thou art our father; we are the clay, and thou our potter; and we all are the work of thy hand" (KJV).

The words of the song sound pretty, don't they?

Pottery.

It starts with a lump of clay, a plan, and a purpose.

The clay is set atop a potter's wheel. As the wheel begins to spin, the potter splashes it with water to give the surface a slippery and workable molding texture, a step that must be repeated throughout the molding process. Then, the potter places his hands in and around the clay as it spins, and as he continues to fold his hands around the material, the lump begins to take shape. Once the clay is lengthened, the potter must very carefully place his hands inside the vessel and gently extend his fingers to bring the desired contour to the outer edges, all the while strengthening the form from the outside and checking the diameter with calipers. The form must be estimated to a certain percentage larger than the final is intended, to compensate for the shrinkage that occurs during drying and firing.

A knife is brought in toward the end of the shaping process to cut excess clay from the base, and then the piece is left alone for a while in order to begin hardening. Before it's completely hardened, however, the potter will revisit the vessel with his turning tools, cutting into the clay flesh—sometimes deeply so—to bring more definition and beauty to the overall design, as well as to smooth out any last imperfections.

From there, the potter sculpts any handles and glues them on. If the end product requires a lid, that is sculpted at this point as well. One false or abrasive move at any previous step until this point could potentially ruin the form entirely. If even one finger presses against the flesh just a bit too hard, it will appear as a dent, and sometimes only after the piece has been fired. Then, the piece is left alone once again, to dry and further harden.

The potter then uses glaze or enamel paints to give decorative patterns on the skin.

If he were to stop there, he would have a lovely—yet likely useless—piece.

In order for the vessel to hold any strength so it can be used for its intended purpose, the clay must now be placed in a firing oven called a kiln and heated at extreme temperatures (over a thousand degrees Celsius, temperatures varying based on the pottery sizes and techniques used: porcelain, stoneware, earthenware, etc.) for typically around eight to sixteen hours (also depending on the firing medium: gas, electric, firewood, kerosene, etc.). This step in the process is very tricky. Some glazes used will melt if the temperature is too high or if they are left in the oven for too long; other glazes will melt if the temperature is not high enough or they are removed from the kiln too quickly. The clay itself will crack if the temperature and length of firing is not exact.

During the firing, the intense heats activate the pigments in the paints, and make the colors come alive…turning what was once a lump of clay into not only a work of art, but also a useful vessel.

When people gather on Sunday morning and sing "You are the Potter, I am the clay; mold me and make me, this is what I pray," do they have any idea what they're actually praying for? Do they have deep understanding of what that process entails?

It is just my opinion that many of them do not. As if being molded like clay into useful pottery is an easy, gentle, and immediate thing. In fact, what we ask for when we sing that song is to be pressed, slathered or smothered in water, spun, pressed again, forced to extend into new shapes, made to feel like we are alone during periods of drying and hardening, shrunken, cut deeply, compelled to stand still while fitted with new handling features, and glazed with suffocation and confusion. And, just when we think we can't take anymore, we are thrust into intense heat for an extensive period of time.

If people only knew what they were asking for, would they still appeal to God for it? Many likely *would*. Why? Because otherwise, they will remain a lump of clay, forever filled with potential, but never utilized or brought to fruition. Sadly, however, acknowledging a list of upcoming challenges and going through the fire are two different things, and it is then that discouragement and debilitation sets in.

What we can't see in the midst of the molding is that while we are being changed, we are being handled by the gentlest Supreme Sculptor. The Master Potter. The One who knows exactly how much pressure we can take before we are forever dented. The One Who knows precisely how much heat we can withstand, and for what length of time we can endure, before we crack. The One Who begins a good work and Who will be faithful to complete it. The One Who knows our usefulness before we were ever formed (Jeremiah 1:5).

Every cut, every pressure, every *flame* was planned in His perfect and artistic will before we ever hit the wheel.

My life story began as a little girl playing pony rides in the neighborhood and performing "surgery" on stuffed animals with my sister. I was no more and no less than any other lump of clay brought into this world, ready for shaping.

Tragedy befell in my early teens and took two of the most central people in my world away from me. I felt the pressure. I felt the sharp turning tools cutting into my form and completely redefining my person at every angle. And when I felt alone, I hardened.

By the time I had reached the age at which a lot of people are discovering their own identities, I had children, a husband, a full-time ministry, and a full-time business, and my shape, my mold, was a blur. I was forced to stand still while I was fit with my handling features—my harness. Every time the fog began to lift, I was slathered in another layer of life's confusing glaze.

When the flames of the ministry's difficulties surrounded me, I nearly thought I would crack in the intense heat. But it was in those moments that the pigments of my true colors were brought to life.

Perhaps the most misunderstood reflection within this historical pottery analogy is the idea that when we are finally crafted, we are finished, and the journey is over. We've been put through the fire and we will arrive on the other side at rest. Nothing could be farther from the truth! Yes, you may have "arrived" at one destination, finally pulled from the heat and allowed to cool, but the journey continues. It is only when you have been constructed as a tool that you are finally ready to be utilized!

In the introduction to this book, we visited the notion that although our shape can be viewed by others around us, that does not always dictate what's developing on the inside. We have the outside of the pottery that people can make speculations about, but only the Master Potter knows what is within us, what we are built to carry, and what our true potential in His Kingdom will be.

The "body of Christ" is a well-known term referring to the Christian church. Its origin is found Paul's writing of 1 Corinthians. "Now you are Christ's body, and individually you are members of it" (12:27; NIV). For centuries since, followers of Christ have striven to be the best participant they can be within this body. But the roles one plays in this endeavor can be confusing.

A talented speaker in my local area once made a profound point regarding our concepts of being within the body of Christ. "Maybe you are the brain," he said. "You have all the answers, and you are in charge, responsible for directing every other body part. But do not be arrogant in this position. You are no more important than any other part. For what good is a brain without the use of limbs or fingers?" He went on later to meet others where they were as well. "Maybe you're the heel of the foot. You feel surrounded by darkness always, you have so much weight placed on top of you, and you feel your position is frequently overlooked. But do not doubt yourself. You are no less important than any other part. For what good is the body if it cannot stand? What destruction awaits if the body loses balance and falls to the ground?"

At times it is easy to assume that you are outshined by great gifts and glamour. You see others around you who "have it all together," who "know what it's all about," who have "arrived." In contrast to these, you may, like myself, assume at one point or other that your own value and dreams pale in comparison. You may wonder if you're merely a simple jar next to a breathtaking, beautifully painted plate. But don't assume that everything you hear about your own value and dreams is true. That plate very well may look beautiful on the outside, but if its sole purpose is to sit high above all others on a plate stand and impress passersby with dazzling appearance, its usefulness remains stunted.

There is something to be said about the simple jars.

When Christ turned the water into wine during the wedding at Cana in Galilee, interestingly enough, He did *not* choose to use the most impressive-looking utensils. He could have made wine appear in any dish or container on the property. For that matter, He could have snapped His fingers and brought from thin air the most glistening vessels made of gold. Read, however, that He used "six stone water jars, the kind used by the Jews for ceremonial washing, each holding from eighty to a hundred and twenty litres [twenty-one to thirty-two US liquid gallons]" (John 2:6; NIV). The same jars that the Jews would cleanse themselves in before conducting a ritual. Why? Because they were the most *useful* for His purpose. He didn't fill a few shiny glasses. When Christ set out to fill a vessel with His gift, He chose the plain, stone jar capable of carrying far more than a small, pretty cup.

For me, Tink changed everything. Her sale was pitched to me as the prettiest gravy boat in the china cabinet. Right? The piece placed proudly at the center of the table to which all other dishes admired. When I got her home, her luster proved to be hidden under a layer of dust, of mystery, and there was a season I was convinced that she had been broken to the point that only pieces of her original usefulness remained.

But I was wrong.

Again, the Lord used a stone jar for his purpose. It wasn't the church, it wasn't a self-help group, and it wasn't an ordained minister. It was an abused, frumpy, bench-legged miniature horse that helped me understand it all. Had I discarded her as her previous owner had, I would have missed out on experiencing not only *her* great reveal, but *my own*…

While I was working with Tink, Jenny, one of my closest friends today, fell upon hard times with her father. She had to sell almost everything she had, uproot her life, and care for him during sickness. Ellie was Jenny's prized miniature horse. She had been house-trained to walk into crowded buildings and visit with people in person as a therapy horse. It appeared as if there was nothing this horse couldn't do. To some minis, as stated in the last chapter, a trailer was a huge mouth, a great threat. But Ellie could take an elevator to the top floor of a hospital, walk down narrow hallways, and press her nose into the hands of the injured, the ill, and the disabled, without a hint of fear.

Before Ellie, I had never even considered using a horse for this purpose. At best, my idea of reaching people for the lost through a horse might have been to let them ride while we visited, which not only paved the way for a very limited ministry endeavor, but it was also exclusive of the very people Ellie was reaching on a daily basis.

When Jenny told me she had to sell Ellie in order to care for her father, I didn't hesitate to buy her. And in owning Ellie, God opened my eyes to a whole world of possibilities, ways to love people and reach them for His Kingdom. A thought that I hadn't fathomed prior.

I remember working with Tink and seeing Ellie prancing about the land. In the same way that I had a significant moment of contemplation while comparing Tink to Cameo, it occurred to me one day that I had a unique opportunity to use my gifts, to reach my potential and realize my life long equine wiring.

I had three fields on my land: a top field, a bottom field, and a middle field. The horses had primarily been allowed access to the middle field to graze. When the grass had all but disappeared from that area, I knew it was time to move them. None of the horses I owned at the time had ever set hoof on the lower field, but they had their own way of letting me know they were all aware of the fresh grass on the other side. I headed to the gate and started unstrapping the chain. Tink heard this, looked at me, and carefully stepped a little closer. She was always watching me to see what I would do. I had already harnessed her a few times, but we hadn't bonded a hundred percent at this point, so as usual, she stood still and regarded me with caution. It was clear that she didn't want me near her, but the field of dreams lay just on the other side of me, and I wasn't moving.

"You want that fresh grass, don't you?" I asked, eyeing her thoughtfully. She stared.

I stared back.

It was either going to be a stand-off of wills, or a twinkling of trust, and I knew I had the patience to wait it out. Gently, so as not to spook her, I opened the gate just wide enough for her to pass, but narrow enough that she would be within my reach should she choose to advance.

"There it is," I said. "All the fresh grass you can eat. Ripe. Green. A whole pasture buffet there for the taking… But you have to get close enough to me to walk through the gate and enjoy it. Are you willing?"

At first, she didn't move. She merely remained stationary, observing me to see if I would open the gate further.

I refused to do so.

If Tink wanted the gift I had for her, she was going to have to trust me enough to accept the gift in the way I was offering it. She was going to have to throw her worries aside long enough to achieve the freedom and goodness awaiting on the other side.

After about a minute, the stare-down came to an end.

Unbelievably, that mare did the last thing I expected her to do. One step first. Then another. Slowly, she came closer and closer until she was within reach. I didn't dare touch her. I just wanted her to know it was safe to be within close proximity to the one who truly loved her. Cautiously, she made her way to the gate, and then through it, one gloriously trusting baby stride at a time. As soon as she was officially past me, she took off like a streak of wild lightning, running with the speed of a racer, jumping with pure joy and freedom over the hills and about the countryside like a lifelong caged bird set loose into the heavens for the first time.

I threw my head back and laughed, cheered for her, clapped, and sang praises behind her for taking the risk that led to her independence from the past. She galloped all over the place with pure abandon. I had rarely seen such a reaction from her, and before I knew it, every other horse was following suit.

It wasn't just her own freedom from the middle field she had inaugurated. Right behind her, like an oncoming train, came every horse on my land. All of them fled into the lower field and ran about, enjoying the grass, the sunshine, galloping about like a majestic equine party.

Another lesson had begun to weave itself into my thoughts.

My eyes swept the landscape and spotted Ellie.

I stopped laughing and clapping.

Something—or rather, *Someone*—was trying to tell me something, and I was bound to be receptive. Having just learned the lesson of being the listener instead of the speaker, I watched from a distance, and waited to hear from that small, *profound* voice that whispered to me in the stillness of the barn.

Ellie was everything that Tink wasn't. Ellie was a nurturer, loved people, loved to be touched, and thrived in an atmosphere where loneliness dominated as a tool for therapy and companionship. Ellie could touch peoples' hearts when and where they needed it, in ways humanity would not. Ellie was the dawning of a new day. Ellie was a *ministry…*

I beheld Tink with her mane flowing about in the celebratory dance of liberty. I watched as all the other mini horses in the lower field were following her. She was new. She was free. She was the leader.

And then the scrambling of contemplation finally settled. Peace fell over me. Truth crept its way into my mind. I started to cry.

I heard the Lord's words.

Nita, if I can bring a miniature horse out of her debilitating and internal confinement, I can do the same for you. I am not through with you yet. You have a ministry ahead of you. A personal one. One you don't even realize you've been praying for all your life. Put yourself out there. I am the Potter. You are My clay. I'm molding you. I'm making you. And I will not place into My vessels more than they can carry, for I am the Master Handler.

And there it was.

The Creator of the universe had a plan for me.

There had been a day when I finally had to grow beyond the mental crippling that past tragedy had inflicted upon me, and move beyond that disability if I was ever going to be utilized to my full potential as a person. It was as if the Lord was giving me the same plea I had given Tink, saying in His gentle way, "Alright, Nita. Here's the deal. I'm not your abuser. I never have been. All I have done is loved you. Now you have to let me harness you for your gifts and service to Me at some point or other, despite what others have done to you. I *chose* you, bought you, and paid for you with My own blood, because I saw the value in you. I still see value in you, despite all you've been through. You *can* make it through this. If you can't stand still and be harnessed, the talents I've instilled in you can't be used. You came from a hard situation, and now you need to realize that you're loved. Do you really want to be stuck in this level of growth? Is that what you want? You're worth so much more than this. Come on, now, Nita. Let's do this. Okay? We can do this. You and Me."

I always innately knew that I would have limitless value to the Lord because I was His creation, His little pal, His little "Cameo." Unlike Cameo, however, the reason I was stifled—my "stifle disease"—had been a result of past trauma, like Tink. "Always loved, but never fully utilized for His purposes" was not written on my branding iron. Yet, although I was aware He wanted me to move beyond, to *harness* my capabilities for His use, it took a lot of processing His love to restore to my potential.

He had *always* had a plan for me.

The dance of liberty was mine. I merely had to trust the Potter that I was on the cooling side of the kiln. Not because I was impenetrable, or that people were any more trustworthy in nature and there would never be another disappointment, but because I was stronger now. While I was in the fire, I didn't crack. I had been handled by the Master Potter, Who knew exactly what He was doing each time he allowed me to feel the sting of change and spiritual maturity. My true colors were alive.

I am now living the life I always wanted. I have beautiful grown children with well-behaved and well-balanced grandkids. Today I have dozens of miniature horses, all of which display their own unique brand of potential. The mission of Whispering Ponies Ranch is to provide the best therapy horse training and placement services as well as facilitating on-site retreats and programs for those who need it most.

Today I am at yet another crescendo in my waltz. God is not through with me yet. Contrarily, He may just be getting started.

I don't know where you are personally in the journey. Perhaps you are in the heat and you feel suffocated. Maybe you are on the other side, cooling, and your great revelation is about to be whispered. Possibly you are a young lump of clay just waiting for the Potter to begin His good work in you, but you fear what is coming.

I'm not going to lie to you. There's a reason you so often hear that life is not easy. It is not meant to be easy. If it were, we would be weak. Stunted. *Stifled.*

It's about the dream. It's about having value when the world says you no longer do. It's about timing. It's about dancing the dance. It's about grounding yourself. It's about learning so many things at once that you're overwhelmed, feeling you'll never understand what you're being taught, and then finally piecing it together on the other side.

You are not forced to ask for the Potter to change you. That is a decision that you, alone, can make. The Holy Spirit is a gentleman, and He will not coerce you into maturity. And who knows? Maybe your life will be cozier without growth. But without growth, you risk never experiencing the reward of achieving your greatest goals or dreams. You risk being shelved. Always *loved* by God, but never *used* by Him to your fullest potential.

If you want to reach the top of your own ladder of capability, you have to climb to get there.

And, if you *do* pray that the Lord touch you, mold you, make you, and develop you, understand what you are asking for.

You may be asking to go through great times of trial, to be stretched uncomfortably. You are giving God the "go-ahead" to test the limits of your fortitude in every facet of your life from every angle imaginable.

But, during those times, remember there is a lesson to be learned at each turn, sometimes from the most unlikely of places, and the strength that will be gained in the fire is invaluable. And now I bring this all to *you*, because *you* aren't done yet.

Trust that the Handler knows who He is handling.

Don't be like Cocoa Puff. Get out there and use your limbs beyond your mental fears. You have more value now with the molding you have gained than you would have been as a lump of potential in the waiting. The concept that you have lost value because of the hits you've taken on the voyage is a lie from the enemy. If you're living in an environment that constantly presses you down, put yourself out there. Surround yourself with change despite the risk.

I don't like to tell my own story. It's painful and unflattering. Yet, it's because of trekking through all of that and being willing to share it that I have made significant connections with others.

Look at Christ. His story was excruciating, and He had many enemies. He wasn't popular. He didn't hobnob with those in authority. He
trekked through the unthinkable and his earthly reward was unimagi-
nable torture and death. The details of His life can be uncomfortable to
read. But *He* faced the fear, allowed *Himself* to be the greatest Vessel, and
now His stands as the most beautiful and life-changing story in history.

You are the clay in the Potter's hands.

What are *you* being molded into?

Be blessed in your own journey. Never believe the lie that your age
or stage of life has anything to do with your usefulness. Whether you are
just being placed on the wheel with your whole life ahead of you, or you
are on the other side of the fire believing that you've arrived, your story is
not over. You are merely at one destination among many, and He always
has a purpose for those who are willing to be sent.

Embrace the lessons. Love on your family. Trust in God's timing.
Know when to believe in the Pink Pony, and when to drive on by. Give
a hand to the man in the mud. Risk trading in your Shorty and Little
One for the unknown as you feel led. Listen to the silence of your brass
clock, and learn to let go of the past. Rearrange your priorities when
your Sundance demands too much. Revisit your concepts of the dream
when your five big horses and one big injury reveal that God knows the
desires of your heart better than you do. Once in a while, stop talking,
and *listen*.

Dance the dance of freedom.

And the waltz goes on.

Whispering Ponies
Ranch Retreat Center

As mentioned early in this memoir, my journey—and the vision and love God gave me for horses and how these beautiful, majestic animals can be used to provide therapy and healing—eventually led to the purchase of 150 acres in Missouri. It is on this land that Whispering Ponies Ranch (WPR) serves as a general retreat facility, as well as a premier training location that specializes in using and gifting therapy animals (horses and dogs). (Construction is nearly finished as this book heads to the printer.) These animals are utilized for ministry at WPR and, by extension, across the nation through a therapy-animal donation program that benefits other care facilities, schools, and ministries.

In 2016, the WPR lodge—a beautiful building constructed in a private setting that can house groups of approximately fifty people—will begin service. The main large training arena (commercial facility) is already done and substitutes as a multipurpose building and auditorium when necessary. Industrial paddocks and watering systems for the animals are now complete, as are public bathrooms, an RV Park, horse-driving and riding paths, prayer-walking trails, a large pond where kids and adults can fish, and more. Early in 2016, we will present a special network television report on SkyWatch TV showing everything that is finalized and available for use at no cost to specialized groups that attend by invitation. Of course, SkyWatch TV's gospel outreach and Whispering Ponies Ranch Retreat Center's hands-on healing ministry are being completed as funds (including personal) are available. The mission of the retreat and media outlet is to provide outreach, recovery, love, rest, healing, learning, and fellowship.

HOW CAN YOU HELP SKYWATCH TV AND WPR RETREAT CENTER?

1. PRAY FOR THIS MINISTRY! Ask the Lord to keep us on track and to maximize His will through what we know He has called us to do in these late hours.
2. PURCHASE BOOKS AND OTHER MEDIA FROM OUR ONLINE STORE! This is currently our main income source paying for operations, equipment, and construction. Every time you buy something from our web store you are investing directly in real ministry. The store address is: http://www.SkyWatchTVStore.com/
3. MAKE A TAX-DEDUCTIBLE DONATION! Please consider making a monthly donation or a one-time gift to Whispering Ponies Ranch or SkyWatchTV. The donate address is http://skywatchtv.com/donate/

Questions? Feel free to contact me through the contact link at our main website here: http://skywatchtv.com/

Mom and Dad.

Mom and Clarence.

My sister Althia.

Baby pic of me.

Me.

Me riding a springy-jumpy horse between my brothers John and Terry.

Check out my haircut!

My sister Althia sleeping with
her baby doll.

Couldn't play the piano but
loved trying.

Crazy horse Coco laying on his mattress.

Me waiting for my brother John to get off Coco so I
could ride him.

This is one of our champion-bloodline miniature stallions. We call him Spot.

And another of our blue ribbon stallions. This guy is named Cowboy.

Check out this beautiful stallion. His name is Hoss

One of our therapy horses. This little girl is the second smallest miniature horse in the world at 18-inches."

A recent picture of me with Chigger at a fair.

More Whispering Ponies Ranch therapy pals—Bucky, Little Red, Diamond, and Stunner.

Therapy horse Two-Tone in gear.

Therapy horse Onyx getting ready.